A Year of Faith and Philosophy

EXPLORING SPIRITUAL GROWTH THROUGH THE LITURGICAL CYCLE

VANCE G. MORGAN

Copyright © 2025 Vance G. Morgan

All rights reserved. No part of this book may be reproduced, stored in a retrieval system, or transmitted in any form or by any means, electronic or mechanical, including photocopying, recording, or otherwise, without the written permission of the publisher.

Unless otherwise noted, the Scripture quotations are from New Revised Standard Version Bible, copyright © 1989 National Council of the Churches of Christ in the United States of America. Used by permission. All rights reserved worldwide.

Church Publishing
19 East 34th Street
New York, NY 10016
www.churchpublishing.org

Cover design by Newgen
Typeset by Nord Compo

ISBN 978-1-64065-778-6 (paperback)
ISBN 978-1-64065-779-3 (eBook)

Library of Congress Control Number: 2024947705

*To the Living Stones adult education seminar,
Trinity Episcopal Church, Pawtuxet, RI*
"Like living stones, let yourselves be built into a spiritual house,
to be a holy priesthood, to offer spiritual sacrifices acceptable
to God through Jesus Christ." 1 Peter 2:5

We are storytelling creatures because we are fashioned in the image of a storytelling God. May we never neglect that gift. May we never lose our love for telling the story.

Nadia Bolz-Weber

Table of Contents

Acknowledgments xi
Prelude and Preliminaries xiii
   The challenge of sacred texts xiv
   Stories and rhythms xvii
   The basics xviii
   Before we begin xix

1. **Advent—What May We Hope For?** 1
   First Sunday of Advent: Keep awake! 2
   Second Sunday of Advent: Prepare the way 5
   Third Sunday of Advent: The Lord is with you 8
   Fourth Sunday of Advent: The strong and silent type 11

2. **Christmas Season—God Made into Flesh** 15
   Christmas Day: What really happened? 16
   Christmas Day: Putting skin on 18
   First Sunday After Christmas Day:
      "In the beginning was the Word" 21
   Second Sunday After Christmas Day:
      A different Christmas story 24
   Second Sunday After Christmas Day:
      Jesus goes about His Father's business 27

3. **Epiphany—Jesus's Coming Out Party** 31
   Epiphany of the Lord 32
   First Sunday After Epiphany: The baptism of Jesus 35
   Second Sunday After Epiphany: The wedding at Cana 37
   Third Sunday After Epiphany: "Today . . . in your hearing" 40
   Fourth Sunday After Epiphany: "Blessed are . . ." 44
   Fifth Sunday After Epiphany: "The light of the world" 47
   Sixth Sunday After Epiphany: "You can make me clean" 50
   Seventh Sunday After Epiphany: "Be perfect" 53
   Eighth Sunday After Epiphany: "Consider the lilies" 55
   Transfiguration Sunday: "Listen to Him" 58

4. **Lent—Beauty for Ashes** 61
   Ash Wednesday: "To dust you shall return" 62
   First Sunday in Lent: Temptation 64
   Second Sunday in Lent: "God so loved the world." 68
   Third Sunday in Lent: Wells of water 71
   Fourth Sunday in Lent: The prodigal son 73
   Fifth Sunday in Lent: The raising of Lazarus 75

5. **Holy Week—From Hosanna to Sepulcher** 79
   Palm Sunday: From palms to Passion 79
   Monday of Holy Week: "You always have the poor" 82
   Tuesday of Holy Week: Righteous anger 84
   Wednesday of Holy Week: Betrayal or denial? 87
   Maundy Thursday: "Could you not keep awake one hour?" 90
   Good Friday: "Actually, he died" 92
   Holy Saturday: "Mortals die, and are laid low." 95

6. **Easter—Everything Has Changed** 99
   Easter: Now it begins 100
   Easter: Getting Jesus out of the tomb 102
   Second Sunday of Easter: A doubting disciple 105
   Third Sunday of Easter: "We had hoped" 108
   Fourth Sunday of Easter: The good shepherd 111
   Fifth Sunday of Easter: When the rules change 113
   Sixth Sunday of Easter: "Do you want to be made well?" 116
   Ascension Sunday: Passing the baton 118
   Pentecost: "The rush of a violent wind" 121
   Trinity Sunday: Celebrating life 124

7. **Ordinary Time—Parables and Miracles** 127
   Proper 4: Do I matter? 128
   Proper 5: Follow me 130
   Proper 6: The fruit of the spirit 133
   Proper 7: Jesus and family values 135
   Proper 8: The fertility of silence 138
   Proper 9: Blessed with a burden 140
   Proper 10: The Good Samaritan 143
   Proper 11: Sowing and reaping 145
   Proper 12: The Kingdom of Heaven is like 148
   Proper 13: Feeding the five thousand 150
   Proper 14: Walking on water 153

Proper 15: Jesus has a bad day 156
Proper 16: This teaching is difficult. 158
Proper 17: Moving past tradition 161
Proper 18: Like a tree 163
Proper 19: Radical forgiveness 166
Proper 20: The last will be first. 168
Proper 21: Delegating authority 171
Proper 22: Jesus and children 173
Proper 23: An inconvenient faith 176
All Saints Sunday: How to become a saint 178
Proper 25: Prosper the work of our hands 181
Proper 26: Wherever you go. 183
Proper 27: Where to find me 186
Proper 28: A different voice 188
Proper 29: The reign of Christ 191

Postlude: Peace be to you. 195
Notes 197
For Further Reading 213

Acknowledgments

A good deal of the material in this book grew from the seeds planted in my blog, *Freelance Christianity: Philosophy, Faith, and the Real World*, which I reluctantly began in the fall of 2012 at the suggestion of a number of trusted friends. Regular writing for the blog has become a spiritual practice. My sincere thanks to my regular and occasional readers—your support, critiques, and commentary have both enriched and energized my spiritual journey. The blog can be found at https://www.patheos.com/blogs/freelancechristianity/.

Much love and many thanks to Mike and Suzy Tkacik, who both read and commented on the first full draft of this book. We have been friends and confidants for more years than any of us care to count—I will cherish forever our conversations around your table during our many visits. The two of you are the only reason that makes me want to visit Florida!

Every writer wishes for an excellent editor but seldom gets one. Fiona Hallowell at Church Publishing has been a writer's dream—her vision of what this book could be beyond what it was when she read the first draft has been the driving force behind the revisions that made it a much better book. Many thanks!

I have been blessed to know and be friends with several Episcopal priests whose wisdom, insights, and support have been integral to my spiritual evolution. Thanks to the late Marsue Harris, Mitch Lindeman, and Tanya Watt for your friendship, commitment to spiritual leadership, and wise insights.

None of this book would have seen the light of day without Jeanne DiPretoro, the beautiful person with whom I have had the joy of spending the past thirty-five years and counting. She has been my first reader, most insightful critic, and a tireless cheerleader for this book from its earliest versions to the finished product. In Plato's *Symposium*, Aristophanes says that our earliest human ancestors were split in half and scattered to the four winds by Zeus in a fit of annoyance; each of us has been driven ever since to find our lost half. I am thankful that we found each other in my parents' living room more than thirty-five years ago.

This book is dedicated to the Living Stones seminar group, a collection of mature and experienced New England Episcopalians at Trinity Episcopal in Pawtuxet, Rhode Island. Defying all stereotypes and odds, "The Stoners" have over the past twelve years been the most welcoming, honest, and loving discussion group I have ever encountered. Anneke, Ann, Cathi, Donna, Laurie, Marge, Nancy, Vicki, and the rest . . . there are very few portions of this book that did not begin in conversations with you. I love you guys!

Prelude and Preliminaries

One sunny morning in September 1983, when I was struggling in my late twenties with serious financial problems, a failing marriage, years of graduate school ahead of me, and a general malaise both spiritual and physical, I wandered into a Sunday morning service at Saint Matthew's Episcopal Cathedral in Laramie, Wyoming. In a rush of emotional response to the beautiful organ, the stately procession of choir, crucifer, deacon, and priest from back to front, and the overwhelming expressions of welcome from dozens of strangers, I felt that I had stumbled into a home whose existence I had not been aware of but for which I had been longing my whole life.

Over the succeeding weeks and months, Saint Matthew's became a life preserver in more ways than one; I jumped into the strange and wonderful world of all things Episcopalian and the liturgical calendar with the enthusiasm of a true convert. My commitment deepened as I experienced Advent for the first time, as Christmas liturgies framed the holidays, and as Epiphany revealed Jesus's coming out party and early ministry in new ways. Saint Matthew's became a haven and refuge; before long, I was a daily regular at morning prayer services in the side chapel. Other than on Wednesdays, when the dean showed up so we could celebrate Eucharist, the responsibility for the daily services rotated through the dozen or so regular attendees.

As fate would have it, I came to the Episcopal Church just as a new hymnbook (1982) and a new Book of Common Prayer (1979) had been approved and recently disseminated to congregations. Since each book was the first significantly revised and updated version in at least four decades, everyone, even the dean of the cathedral, was more or less at square one as new and unfamiliar hymns as well as a seemingly endless variety of new possibilities for liturgies were suddenly available.

What was it about liturgical worship that seduced me so thoroughly? Since liturgical worship is framed by texts from the Jewish scriptures and the New Testament, the answers to that question begin with a description of my own religious background and upbringing and how that upbringing shaped my relationship with sacred texts.

The challenge of sacred texts

There are times when I feel as if I were born in church. My father was a Baptist preacher, the cofounder and president of a small Bible school in northern New England that trained pastors to be placed in small-town churches in the northeast that had been closed, sometimes for decades. My mother, older brother, and I travelled with my father in the summer throughout the Northeast and some summers across the country to various Bible conferences where he was the rock star keynote minister. We were his blood-related groupies.

My religious tradition was Protestant, conservative, fundamentalist, evangelical, and as nonliturgical as a religious tradition could possibly be. I often tell the uninitiated that we had Christmas, Easter, and everything else. Advent? Epiphany? Lent? All Saints Day? Never heard of any of them. With the exception of Christmas and Easter, every Sunday was pretty much the same: hymns, prayer, announcements, choir, prayer, hour-long sermon, hymn, prayer.

We believed that the Bible (King James Version, preferably) was the literal and inerrant Word of God, a divinely inspired text that contained all answers to all problems and issues that a person might encounter. God was contained within the leather covers of a book and had said nothing new ever since the Bible was completed. The God of my youth was supposedly loving, but more often was judgmental, aloof, and ready to hold me responsible for the slightest infraction at a moment's notice.

I learned to read at a very early age, so by the time I was six or seven years old I annually embarked on a "Through the Bible in a Year" reading project that only the most dedicated youngsters at our church took on. Guided by a small pamphlet that was distributed early each January, I read a few chapters each morning and evening, not so much for comprehension or edification as for gaining brownie points with God. I spent twelve to fifteen weeks per year memorizing scripture verses, then reciting them to my "hearer" (who was usually my aunt) on Sunday. At age six, I memorized four verses per week. By the time I was in high school, I was memorizing as many as fifteen verses per week, often one extended passage. All of the young folk did this. I don't remember anyone particularly complaining about this forced memorization, neither do I recall that anyone enjoyed it. It was simply a rite of passage—one that deposited hundreds of Bible texts in my memory files by the time I went to college.

It truly wasn't until I was in my early thirties and entered the college classroom as a newly minted professor for the first time that I began to realize just how deeply the Bible had shaped me. I had stopped believing that the book is the literal "Word of God" years before, but its stories, lessons, quirks, contradictions, rants, genealogies, wild and crazy prophecies, and moralizing were part of my DNA. I'm a philosophy professor, not a theologian or a preacher, so I wasn't using the Bible to preach, proselytize, or convict. I was using it to illustrate the best and worst that human beings can be, the various ways that different cultures over time have sought to understand and describe what is greater than us and our relationship to it. I have continued to do this for the last thirty-five years. There are few classes during which I don't pull something out of my memory banks from the Bible that is relevant to whatever is on the table for discussion.

When advising incoming freshmen at my college on how to best prepare for the large interdisciplinary humanities program that is the centerpiece of our core curriculum, I always say the same thing: "Know your Greek mythology, and know your Bible. Not as the 'Word of God' to be handled reverently with kid gloves, but as arguably the most influential book in the Western literary tradition. You will not be able to understand the literature of the West if you don't know the Bible well."

Away from my professional life as a teacher, my relationship to the Bible is a challenging one to describe. It is not my moral answer book in the way that many people of faith might describe it. It isn't my go-to source for answers to tough questions. My relationship with the Bible is more like my relationship with the weather—it's both as familiar as the air that I breathe and as unpredictable as the wind. It truly is part of me, but not always in ways that I appreciate. I am frequently asked whether I believe that the Bible is "the Word of God." I used to answer, "that depends on what you mean by 'Word' and 'God,'" which didn't turn out to be a very effective response. Now I usually tell stories.

One Sunday evening over forty years ago, I heard a well-known and much-loved Baptist minister, a family friend and the godfather of my firstborn son, say something shocking from the pulpit. He lifted his well-worn Bible above his head in his right hand and proclaimed, "This is not the Word of God!" Gasps filled the sanctuary, followed by an uncomfortable silence. After a dramatic pause of several moments, he continued. "This is just ink on paper between leather covers. This is just a book. This becomes the Word of God when the Holy Spirit makes it so to each of us individually."

My son's godfather was right. The divine word changes and grows in each of us, often in apparent conflict with what we thought was already fixed and settled. When temptations arise to find security and safety in inflexible interpretations of scripture, it is worth taking the words of Paul to the church at Corinth to heart: "The letter kills, but the Spirit gives life."

Stories and rhythms

Although I was raised to revere the Bible, a reverence that bordered on worship, it wasn't until I encountered liturgical worship that is shaped by selected lectionary readings that I came to fully appreciate and love the Bible in its totality. In my experience, those who treat the Bible as essentially the fourth member of the Trinity tend to be very selective in the portions that they emphasize, tending equally to deemphasize or completely ignore obviously contradictory or stubbornly obscure passages.

In the lectionary readings that ground liturgical worship, no portions of scripture are considered too problematic or unimportant for public display. In a given Sunday gospel reading Jesus is as likely to call a foreign woman a dog or speak dismissively to his mother as he is to tell a compelling parable or raise someone from the dead. The depressing psalms get as much play as the joyful ones. The prophets rage about how disappointingly disobedient the people of Israel are while also promising God's continuing protection and love, despite appearances. God acts like a toddler in one passage and as a wise and beloved parent in the next.

Simply listening and attending to what is read from the lectern for a year of Sundays exposes one to an inexhaustible range of possibilities about the relationship between human beings and what is greater than us. The whole range of human emotions and commitments is on display, most often packaged within stories. And this makes sense, since storytelling is in our human DNA. Stories are the natural context within which human beings understand themselves and each other; it is no surprise that Jesus was an incurable storyteller.

The lectionary readings are selected to mirror the rhythms of the liturgical calendar; these rhythms reflect the natural human orientation to both change and stability, just as the texts resonate with our natural attunement to stories and narratives. The change of seasons, birth and death, what the ancients used to call "generation and corruption"—within definitive and stable parameters, things are constantly and cyclically changing. The stories and rhythms of the liturgical year will become more and more apparent as we proceed. First, though, it is important to first take a look at the lay of the land that we will be exploring.

The basics

Since it is easy to get lost in the trees of the liturgical calendar, let's begin with a 30,000-foot view of the forest, a view that provides the general organization of this book. I am most familiar with how the Episcopal Church organizes the liturgical year and its lectionary readings, so that is the framework I will be using in this book. Catholic, Orthodox, and Protestant Christians other than Episcopalians will be aware of various differences that, although important, are not crucial for our present discussion.

The liturgical year has seven seasons: Advent, Christmas, Epiphany, Lent, Holy Week, Easter, and Ordinary Time. Some of these seasons are always the same length (Christmas, Lent, Holy Week, Easter) while the length of the other seasons varies depending on moveable dates like Thanksgiving and Easter.

The Revised Common Lectionary provides a three-year cycle (A, B, and C) of readings for Sundays and feast days, with a separate two-year cycle (One and Two) for weekdays. I will be focusing exclusively on the Sunday lectionary readings throughout this book, plus a few additional special days such as Epiphany, Ash Wednesday, and the weekdays of Holy Week.

Each new liturgical year begins with the First Sunday of Advent (usually the first Sunday after Thanksgiving unless the holiday comes early). The readings for each Sunday of the liturgical year include a reading from the Jewish scriptures, a psalm, a New Testament reading (usually from one of the letters), and the gospel text; there frequently are two possibilities to choose from except for the gospel reading. The Gospels of Matthew, Mark, and Luke are the focus of the Sunday gospel readings in years A, B, and C respectively, with John's gospel occasionally showing up in all three years.

In what follows there is a section for each possible Sunday of the liturgical year. The scripture readings I have chosen to reflect on are selective; scriptures for the relevant passages in each section will be identified by reference and by liturgical year (A, B, or C) after the section title. The chosen passages are intended to whet the reader's appetite for a full exploration of all of the texts available for a given Sunday and liturgical season. When appropriate I occasionally refer to passages from Scripture that are not in a particular Sunday's lectionary selections. My hope is to inspire the reader to become fully immersed in the wealth of riches contained in the Jewish and Christian scriptures.

Before we begin . . .

In the syllabus for every course I have taught over the past twenty years, I have included this: "My job is not to tell you what to think. My job is to get you to think." The same applies to this book. My own understanding of the texts under consideration has evolved over the decades; there is no reason to believe that this evolution will not continue.

Still, there are common themes throughout this book that reflect where I currently find myself as a person of faith. These themes include an emphasis on the humanity of Jesus, a commitment to open-endedness and a suspicion of claims to certainty, the conviction that the divine way of doing things often turns our assumptions and traditions on their heads, and embracing the idea that God's decision to become human, the Incarnation, continues in those of us who seek to follow Jesus. As amazing as it may seem, God has chosen human beings as the primary vehicle of bringing the divine into the world. It is a risky strategy, but one that demonstrates both God's love and God's respect for us. We will be engaging with this remarkable story frequently as we proceed.

One final preliminary consideration: Practice being open to surprise and mystery rather than falling back on familiar and comfortable interpretations. Many of the stories and texts from Scripture are so familiar that we are strongly tempted to think there is nothing new to be learned or experienced, forgetting just how wild and untamable the texts often are. We are strongly tempted to simplify mystery, as writer Sarah Bessey describes in this passage:

> *There are a lot of weird stories we've tamed over the years: floods and rainbows, burning bushes that are not consumed, healings, prophets, talking donkeys, fish with money in their mouths, and widows with inexhaustible oil to sell, the dead rising . . . The number of weird and wondrous happenings in the Bible is staggering. But we've removed wonder to turn God into a manageable deity, a force understandable to our minds and our methods and concerns. We're all seeking to tame the wonder because non-knowing is scary to us.*

For persons of faith, it is important to remember that, first and foremost, God is mystery. The best responses to mystery are wonder, open-endedness, and resistance to premature closure and certainty. With that in mind, Advent calls.

CHAPTER 1

Advent—What May We Hope For?

The First Sunday of Advent, almost always the Sunday following Thanksgiving, is the first day of the new liturgical year. I was raised in a version of Christianity that had no sense of the liturgical year. The landmarks of my Baptist youth were Christmas, Easter, and everything else. I knew nothing of Advent until my twenties, and loved its energy, its carols, its texts. Inwardness, reflection, anticipation, and patience—Advent is for introverts.

Although I have now spent well over half of my life as an Episcopalian, I still find this liturgical and lectionary stuff just as fascinating and compelling today as I did when I first wandered into Saint Matthew's Cathedral in Laramie, Wyoming, more than four decades ago. I love Advent's call to centeredness, to watchfulness, to expectation, its hymns, and its purple.

The great but incredibly difficult German philosopher Immanuel Kant, in a rare moment of clarity, wrote that all important human questions can be boiled down to these three: *What can I know? What ought I to do?* and *What may I hope for?* Advent focuses on the last of these questions.

First Sunday of Advent: Keep awake!

Year A: Isaiah 2:1–5, Romans 13:8–14, Matthew 24:37–44; Year B: Mark 13:24–37

Those in charge of the Episcopal Church I have regularly attended for more than a decade have often been generous enough to let me be the homilist for one Sunday during Advent. Over the years I have chosen the Sundays involving Zechariah, his son John the Baptist, Joseph, and Mary, always fascinated to find how the different Gospels focus on specific and various aspects of these foundational and formative stories.

But I have always stayed away from the First Sunday of Advent. Why? Because although later Advent Sunday texts wrap us up in familiar stories like a well-worn, comfortable blanket, Advent begins with "shock and awe." The message of Advent 1 texts is always, "Get ready for a divine invasion. And if you aren't paying attention, if you aren't prepared, it isn't going to be pretty."

In the Year A reading from the Jewish scriptures, Isaiah prophesies that "they shall beat their swords into plowshares, and their spears into pruning hooks"—and in Matthew's gospel, Jesus advises, "Therefore you also must be ready, for the Son of Man is coming at an unexpected hour." In Mark's gospel, we read that

> *[t]hen they will see the Son of Man coming in clouds with great power and glory . . . But about that day or hour no one knows . . . Beware, keep alert; for you do not know when the time will come . . . Therefore, keep awake, for you do not know when the master of the house will come, in the evening, or at midnight, or at cockcrow, or at dawn, or else he may find you asleep when he comes suddenly. Keep awake.*

A few years ago, I had the opportunity to observe a colleague in class who was seeking promotion. The topic of the lecture was various aspects of postmodern philosophy, a topic that promised to stun all those in attendance, myself included, into soporific silence. But my colleague knew what he was doing. He started with the opening minutes from the 2004 British zombie comedy *Shaun of the Dead*, which has become a cult classic. Shaun, an electronics store employee with girlfriend problems, no respect at work, deadbeat friends, and no direction in his life, leaves his flat in London one morning to walk a few blocks to the local convenience store for a Coke and an ice cream cone.

As he shuffles the round trip in a half-aware stupor, he fails to realize that something apocalyptic has happened during the night. The convenience store is empty except for a corpse lying in the aisle, the freezer door he opens to select his ice cream is smeared with blood, and the streets are becoming more and more filled with staggering, half-rotted zombies. There is no significant difference between this unaware person who is completely disengaged from his life and a zombie. And this, the postmodernists tell us, has become the human condition.

Sounds like a good time for Advent, whose call to us is the same as Paul's call to the Romans: "[I]t is now the moment for you to wake from sleep." This waking business has been an issue for me for as long as I can recall. One of my earliest memories is of pretending to sleep in the back of the family car while riding the fifteen miles or so home from Sunday night church. My underlying emotion during that ride was fear. I was afraid that I was going to die and go to hell. I was afraid Jesus would come back and I'd be left behind. I would miss the rapture. I worried that I was not "born again" in the way that I was sure everyone in my family was.

Every Sunday night, as a natural follow-up to the meeting-concluding "altar call" for people to give their lives to Jesus, I would have my own altar call curled up in the corner of the back seat. My greatest fear wasn't going to hell—it was that my whole family would be raptured in the blink of an eye, leaving me and every other "un-born-again" person behind. This haunted me.

If I came home on the bus after school and my mother wasn't where I expected her to be in the house, my first thought was that she'd been raptured. I felt alone even when with lots of other people because they all had something I didn't have—they all belonged, and I didn't.

I got over my rapture-phobia at some point in my adolescence. It's a good thing; otherwise, the Advent 1 readings would scare the crap out of me. For instance, Jesus says this in Matthew's gospel:

> *Two will be in the field; one will be taken and one will be left. Two women will be grinding meal together; one will be taken and one will be left. Keep awake therefore, for you do not know on what day your Lord is coming.*

These texts, apparently intended to frighten us into straightening out our crooked ways, are disturbing. Evangelical minister and author Tim LaHaye and others have made millions cashing in on such fear in the *Left Behind* book series, movies, and accompanying paraphernalia.

Assuming for a moment that Advent isn't about scaring us, what are we really being called to consider with such texts? Something Paul says to the church at Rome is helpful: "You know what time it is . . . the night is far gone, the day is near. Let us then throw off the works of darkness and put on the armor of light." *Wake up!!!* in other words.

The default human condition so often is to sleepwalk through our days, months, and years. The divine word of Advent is that big change is coming. The question is, will we even notice?

> *For reflection: What are the ways in which we sleepwalk through our lives? How might the call of Advent to "Wake up!" be helpful in becoming aware of what one is doing and of who one is?*

Second Sunday of Advent: Prepare the way

Year A: Matthew 3:1–12; Year B: Mark 1:1–8; Year C: Luke 3:1–6, Baruch 5:1–9

The gospel readings for Advent 2 focus on Jesus's relative, John the Baptist. The Gospels of Mark and John begin their narratives not with the stories related to Jesus's birth, but rather with John the Baptist crying in the wilderness. The consistent message of Advent 2 is John the Baptist quoting Isaiah: "Prepare the way of the Lord, make his paths straight."

John the Baptist's miraculous birth is described at the beginning of Luke's gospel. Zechariah had not spoken for months, struck dumb because he found it difficult to believe the angel's announcement that his wife, Elizabeth, well past childbearing years, would bear a son. When Zechariah and Elizabeth's son is circumcised at eight days old, a family squabble breaks out over what the baby's name will be.

Most of the group votes for "Zechariah Junior." But Zechariah motions for a tablet and writes, "His name is John," as the angel directed. His power of speech returns, and Zechariah delivers what has come to be known as the Song of Zechariah or the Benedictus, one of the most beautiful songs in all of Scripture. The Benedictus closes with a meditation on Zechariah's new son's role in the divine economy, followed by a stunning promise:

> *And you, child, will be called the prophet of the Most High,*
> *for you will go before the Lord to prepare his ways,*
> *To give knowledge of salvation to his people*
> *by the forgiveness of their sins.*
> *By the tender compassion of our God,*
> *the dawn from on high will break upon us,*
> *to give light to those who sit in darkness and in the shadow*
>   *of death,*

to guide our feet into the way of peace.

Advent's strongest image is pregnancy. Elizabeth's . . . Mary's . . . so unexpected, so miraculous. A distant, long-promised hope is about to literally be fleshed out. As we turn our attention away from our obsession with the human condition and toward distant promise, we choose to believe that when the divine takes on our human suffering and pain, we in turn take on divinity itself. The choice to look outward in expectation is within our power, as described in the apocryphal book Baruch:

> *Take off the garment of your sorrow and affliction and put on forever the beauty of the glory from God. Put on the robe of the righteousness that comes from God; put on your head the diadem of the glory of the Everlasting; for God will show your splendor everywhere under heaven. For God will give you evermore the name, "Righteous Peace, Godly Glory."*

The phrase "It's always darkest just before the dawn" is usually little more than a platitude, but in this case it makes sense. We have reason to hope because help is on the way. But what sort of help?

In *Philosophical Fragments*, nineteenth-century Danish philosopher Søren Kierkegaard tells a charming story about a powerful king who falls in love with a lowly maiden. The maiden is unaware of the king's love, and the king is worried. Knowing that love is built on equality, how is the gap between his royal greatness and her humble maidenhood to be crossed? He does not want to coerce her into loving him by revealing his love in all of its splendor, nor would elevating her to royal status work, since then she would simply be the same lowly maiden with a better wardrobe and job description.

The only possible solution to the king's problem is remarkably simple. "Since union could not be brought about by an elevation it must be attempted by a descent." The king must step down from his royal throne and enter the maiden's hut as an equal. Not as a king in a peasant's costume, but as a peasant. Only then can he be sure that she might return his love because of the person he is rather than because of the role he inhabits. And this, Kierkegaard reminds us, is precisely the mystery and madness of love, not only of the king for the maiden, but also of God for human beings. "This is the unfathomable nature of love, that it desires equality with the beloved, not in jest merely, but in earnest and truth."

When we try to "make sense" of the Incarnation, to shape the heart of the Christian faith into doctrine, we would do well to remember that the energizing reason for the Incarnation is love—and love is notoriously untheorizable. We know this from human love; to the extent that one tries to explain why one loves another, the love is reduced to something unrecognizable. There is no reason to think that love between God and us will be any easier to get a handle on.

We might start by considering a possibility that we very seldom, if ever, hear about in church. What if we accept God's love for humanity, a love so great that it inspires God to become human, as a sign that we are worth it? Imagine the challenge presented to the king in Kierkegaard's story, who now, as a peasant, must win the love of the maiden whom he inexplicably loves. Surely there will be regular temptations to rely or fall back on what he has left behind—his power, wealth, connections, and status. But if she is to truly love him, she must love him for what he truly is—an ordinary human being just as she is. He must live, work, eat, and sleep in the same world as she does, with no special favor or trappings.

During the Advent season, as we await the Incarnation anew, as we are surrounded by daily reminders of how deeply into apathy, depravity, and evil human beings are capable of descending, it is worth remembering that we are also the recipients of divine love, a love of which, in some inexplicable way, we are worthy. If

God has taken pleasure in divine creation, there is every reason to assume that some part of God's pleasure is in your best idea, your most generous impulse, your most disciplined thinking on whatever is true, honorable, just, pure, pleasing, excellent, and worthy of praise.

For reflection: What difference would it make if you believed that God's becoming human is best framed by believing in human worthiness rather than in human depravity? What are the practical implications of such a reorientation?

Third Sunday of Advent: The Lord is with you

Year A: Isaiah 35:1–10, Matthew 11:2–11; Luke 1:46–55

The gospel readings for Advent 3 continue to focus on John the Baptist's ministry. In Matthew's account, from the final months of John's life, the Baptist sends his disciples to ask his cousin Jesus a "What may I hope for?" question: "Are you the one who is to come, or are we to wait for another?" This is one of the many poignant and excruciatingly human scenes in the Gospels—John has been imprisoned by Herod Antipas and his head will be on a plate soon. He is by no means the only prophet in the land; they came a dime a dozen in those days. Nor is Jesus the only Messiah candidate around—Israel is full of them. John's question is not academic. What he really wants to know is, "Has my whole life been a waste?"

Jesus's answer to John's question relies on John's knowledge of the prophet Isaiah. "Go and tell John what you hear and see: the blind receive their sight, the lame walk, the lepers are cleansed, the deaf hear, the dead are raised, and the poor have good news brought to them." Hopefully the message got back to John before he was executed by Herod. The man whom you baptized is the real deal—the Messiah has truly come. That's what John foretold and what he waited for.

As Christians we anticipate, and eventually celebrate, what we believe to be the single most important event in human history—the Incarnation. But what exactly will we be celebrating when Christmas arrives? What difference do the circumstances of Jesus's birth make, a story told differently by Matthew and Luke and considered to be so insignificant by Mark and John that they don't even include it? As the thirteenth-century Dominican monk Meister Eckhart provocatively asked, "What good is it for me that Christ was born a thousand years ago in Bethlehem?" It's a great question, one that Advent provides us with many opportunities to ask in various ways.

* * *

An optional Year A lectionary reading for Advent 3 is one of the most beloved songs in all of Scripture from Luke's gospel, Mary's Magnificat. From the few details in the Gospels, joined together with what we know about the culture in which Mary lived, we can sketchily picture Mary. Mary is young, most likely twelve or thirteen years old. She is betrothed to Joseph, a man much older than Mary. She is almost certainly poor. Her skin is darker than suggested in traditional artwork. She has dirt under her fingernails. We do not know whether she has siblings, nor do we know from the Gospels anything about her parents. She's nothing special, just an insignificant young girl living in a nothing town in the eastern backwater of the Roman Empire. And she is visited by an angel.

In Scripture, angels are always the heralds of new beginnings, inviting us to adventure. They introduce mystery—they do not clarify. Angels announce new departures and the beginning of something whose end is not in view. This particular angel's announcement to Mary begins with: "Greetings, favored one!

The Lord is with you." And in the narrative of the Incarnation that Advent prepares us for, the Lord is with all of us. "Greetings, favored ones! The Lord is with us."

Most of us are all too aware of our humanity, of our shortcomings and failings—that we bear the burden, as philosopher and theologian John Henry Newman wrote, of "some terrible aboriginal calamity." But we are also the bearers of the divine. The promise to Mary is the promise to us—the Lord is with us. We, as Mary, are the wombs from which the divine enters the world each day. We are the incubators of God. Mary's response to Gabriel is the only one possible—"How can this be?" It is a mystery. It is also a great story.

Why Mary? She knows that she is nothing special, that she has done nothing to earn such favor. The only explanation is love. Love is holy because it is a lot like grace—the worthiness of its object is never really what matters. The astounding mystery and wonder of God's love for us permeates throughout the beautiful story of the Annunciation and the Magnificat that follows. This favor and blessing continues. The story of God's becoming flesh is a direct response to our inherent flaws, imperfections, limitations, and evil. Divine favor and blessing are offered to all of us. That is the mystery, the scandal, and the beauty of the Incarnation story: God entrusts flawed human beings to be the divine in the world.

The Incarnation we anticipate and that is incubating in each of us as Advent proceeds is the moment of salvation as God enters time, history, and each of us. Advent reminds us that in our lives there is always a child ready to enter the world—the divine child that is in each of us and the child of God that each of us is. We all are favored of God, loved by God, regardless of whether we feel it or deserve it. A great gift has been placed in us, a gift that carries with it unlimited responsibility. How will we nurture this child? How will we bring it to birth? What is incubating in each of us is as individual and unique as each of us is—and it is divine. Mary's response in her Magnificat must be ours: "Here we are, the servants of the Lord. Let it be with us according to your Word."

For reflection: Angels in Scripture are the heralds of new beginnings; Advent calls us to be open to new paths and directions. In which places in your life would change and new beginnings be most welcome? Where would they be most challenging?

Fourth Sunday of Advent: The strong and silent type

Year A: Matthew 1:18–25

The birth of Jesus is set up in Matthew's gospel not with the women of the story, Elizabeth and Mary, in central roles, but rather with Joseph, the descendant of David. Scholars tell us that Matthew's primary focus is to convince a Jewish audience that Jesus, this Jewish man who is the central figure in Matthew's narrative, crucified as a common criminal, was actually the promised Messiah. Matthew's intentions are clear from the start when his gospel begins with a genealogy that traces Jesus's ancestry all the way back from his stepfather, Joseph, through King David to Abraham.

It turns out that there are some questionable women in Joseph's family tree. Salmon, David's great-grandfather, for instance, marries Rahab, whose story is told in the book of Joshua from the Jewish scriptures. The invading children of Israel send spies into the Promised Land to scout out the area; they wind up in Jericho, a walled fortress that is the most important and powerful city in Canaan. We find them in the house of Rahab, a prostitute who hides them from the king of Jericho and helps them escape from the city by dropping a rope from her window for them to climb down in the middle of the night.

For her efforts, this non-Israelite prostitute and her family are the only inhabitants of Jericho spared when Joshua and his army, using information from the spies Rahab saved, conquer and destroy Jericho a few chapters later. Another surprising woman in Joseph's lineage is the Moabite widow Ruth, who will marry Boaz, the son of Rahab and Salmon; their story will be considered in a later chapter.

What do we learn from Matthew and from Luke, the only Gospels in which Joseph appears, about Joseph? First, Joseph is the strong, silent type. While other important characters in the stories of Jesus's birth and formative years get major speaking parts, we have no record of Joseph's ever saying anything. In reality, I suspect that he was capable of speech when necessary, but he gets no gospel speaking role.

Second, Joseph is in touch with his inner self in a way that would make modern therapists proud. He pays attention to his dreams and acts on them. In fact, he's perhaps the greatest dreamer in the Bible other than his namesake and distant ancestor Joseph from Genesis. The difference between them is that Genesis Joseph is *not* the strong, silent type, can't stop blabbing about his dreams to everyone, and ends up in a well. Jesus's stepdad knows that some things are meant to be acted on and not talked about.

Third, Joseph clearly is flexible and able to roll with the punches. One would think that the angel Gabriel might have made the annunciation to Mary and Joseph together, but no. Only Mary gets the message. We aren't told if Joseph finds out that Mary is pregnant because she tells him her story or because he happens to notice that she's putting on weight, but because he is a "just man" he chooses to break their betrothal privately rather than making a public display of it as the law would have allowed. Finally, an angel gets around to telling Joseph what's up in a dream, and the betrothal is back on.

In Santa Fe, New Mexico, there is a little church called the Loretto Chapel, located for the past many years on the grounds of a downtown hotel, which contains a "miraculous staircase" built by a stranger with a donkey and a toolbox who showed up in answer to the prayers of the Sisters of Loretto. The newly built chapel needed a staircase to the choir loft; those who knew about such things said it would have to be a ladder, since a regular stairway would be too invasive of the chapel space.

The stranger built an architectural marvel, a spiral staircase containing two 360-degree turns with no visible means of support and held together with wooden pegs rather than nails, then disappeared without being paid after completing the staircase. Legend has it that the donkey-riding stranger was none other than St. Joseph, patron saint of carpenters. This sounds like something that Joseph would do. Something needs to be done, and he does it. After dealing with a pregnant fiancée he's never slept with, dream-talking angels, a murderous king, lost reservations at the inn, delivering a baby in a barn, and being a stepfather, building a staircase that defies gravity for a bunch of nuns is nothing. Bring it on.

For reflection: Joseph was a man of action rather than of words. Think of the ways in which your faith commitment might benefit from a similar focus on action rather than words, on what you do rather than what you say. How might this look?

CHAPTER

2

Christmas Season—God Made into Flesh

The heart of Christmas begins in the silent mystery of the Incarnation and continues in the strange and beautiful ways in which the divine chooses to enter our world in human form on a daily basis. The Christmas season is the shortest of all liturgical seasons, spanning the twelve days from Christmas to Epiphany. Because so many fascinating and important texts are spread throughout the three-year cycle of readings during this season, I have provided two additional readings and reflections for the season, one for Christmas Day and one for the second Sunday after Christmas.

Christians often have discussions, sometimes heated, about which is the most important event at the heart of the Christian faith: what we celebrate at Easter or what we celebrate at Christmas? A strong case can be made for either side of this debate, but I have always been an Incarnation person. It was a new understanding of the Incarnation a number of years ago that brought me out of a spiritual crisis that threatened to move me out of the life of faith altogether.

The stories of Jesus's birth set the stage for the most mysterious and remarkable of claims: God loves humanity so much that God chose to become human to establish the importance of God's divine relationship with us. And God continues to choose human beings as the way to bring the divine into the world. Our response should be gratitude, awe, and disbelief all tangled together, saying with wonder along with Melchior gazing at the manger in *The Nativity Story*, my favorite Christmas movie: "God made into flesh." Remarkably small. Disturbingly fragile. Completely mysterious. And utterly true.

Christmas Day: What really happened?

Years A, B, C: Luke 2:1–20

The primary lectionary text for Christmas liturgies is the familiar nativity story from Luke's gospel, including no room at the inn, angels singing to shepherds, and a baby in a manger. But Luke is the only one of the four canonical Gospels that says anything about Jesus's actual birth, which raises the obvious question—what really happened in Bethlehem over two thousand years ago? And do the historical details really matter?

Christmas movies are a big deal at my house. My wife, Jeanne, goes for the classics, such as *Miracle on 34th Street*, *The Bishop's Wife*, *It's a Wonderful Life*, and (her favorite) *White Christmas*. I tend to favor more recent ones, like *The Holiday*, *Love Actually*, *Joyeux Noël*, and my favorite, *The Nativity Story*. *The Nativity Story* presents a remarkably straightforward and beautiful melding of the narratives from Matthew and Luke. All of the expected elements are there—Elizabeth and Zechariah, Mary and Joseph, shepherds and wise men at the manger, angels in appropriate places saying appropriate things, along with a creepy father-and-son team of Herod the Great and Herod Antipas.

Another classic movie provides some tools for figuring out what really happened on that most important day in the Christian calendar. *Rashomon*, Akira Kurosawa's 1950 film masterpiece that is often mentioned on short lists of "the greatest movies ever," is fascinating for many reasons. But to a philosophy professor who frequently teaches Philosophy of Knowledge courses, its main appeal is that it is an early cinematic exploration of the importance of individual perspective to our understanding of the world around us. Through the ingenious use of camera and flashbacks, Kurosawa reveals the complexities of human nature as four people recount different versions of the story of a man's murder and the rape of his wife.

The viewer is left wondering, "what *really* happened?" and "whose perspective is closest to the truth?" The answer is that we have no idea. Which version of events is most convincing will vary from person to person, depending on many factors; by not providing us with an objective, "God's eye" view of the events in question, Kurosawa immerses the viewer in ambiguity, both fascinating and frustrating.

What makes *Rashomon* disturbing is that its portrayal of the central roles played by subjectivity and ambiguity in the shaping of belief and truth is not just sophisticated entertainment—it is precisely how the "truth" is actually constructed, both individually and collectively, in the "real world." We often claim to be interested in objectivity and facts, but what even counts as a fact is from the beginning shot through with the experiences and lived contributions of each person seeking to know "what really happened."

This leads to radically different interpretations of shared facts; as William James reminds us in his essay "Pragmatism and Humanism":

> *We read the same facts differently. "Waterloo," with the same fixed details, spells a victory for an Englishman; for a Frenchman it spells a defeat.*

Whose interpretation of the battle's events is correct—the Englishman's or the Frenchman's? That question has no "correct" answer, which is problematic because the Battle of Waterloo is close enough to us historically that we should presumably be able to agree on some of the details of what happened. The problems of perspective, interpretation, context, and subjectivity increase exponentially the more distant in time the events in question become.

What really happened in Bethlehem? We have no eyewitness accounts; what we do have in the Gospels, written decades after the event, is remarkably different from gospel to gospel. The authors of Mark and John apparently didn't think the circumstances of Jesus's birth important enough to even report on, while the authors of Matthew and Luke construct their stories from "cherry-picked" details. Luke does not mention the wise men or a star, while Matthew has no worshipping shepherds or even a manger, but wise men following a star visit the Holy Family in a house, probably in Nazareth, sometime after Jesus's birth.

So, where lies the truth? A friend who passed away a few years ago tended to be rather definitive in his pronouncements. Once at lunch he said that "the heart of Christianity is what you believe about the stories. Do you believe the stories are true or don't you? Yes or No? And if you say, 'Let me think about it,' that's the same as saying 'No!'" This was not directed at me specifically—he was just drawing a line in the sand.

But I think I'm in trouble. Because not only am I not sure about whether my answer to his question is "Yes," "No," "Let me think about it," or even "Which stories are you referring to?"—I'm inclined to say, "It doesn't matter." What matters more than the accuracy of the stories is what these stories mean to you and what difference they have made to your life.

For reflection: To what extent does your faith commitment depend on the historical accuracy, the "facts," of what happened on the day that we celebrate at Christmas? Does it matter that we cannot answer these questions with certainty?

Christmas Day: Putting skin on

Toward the end of most fall semesters, I spend a couple of weeks in the New Testament with a classroom full of college freshmen.

One year, knowing that this was a group, largely the product of twelve years of Catholic parochial school education, for whom the Bible in college might be a tough sell, I asked my seminar students an out-of-the-box question right at the start: What difference does it make whether these stories are true or not? If it were definitively proven tomorrow that Jesus never existed, then what?

A fascinating discussion ensued, full of more nuance and insight than even I expected. Contributions ranged across the spectrum of possibilities, but one student's comment particularly stayed with me. "I'd still be a Christian," she said. "Because being a Christian makes me a better person than I would be if I wasn't." That's a good start—the measure of one's faith is what impact it has in real time on the life being lived.

The story of the Incarnation, of God out of love becoming human, is not about facts. It is a framework for believing that we matter enough to be loved by what is greater than us, and that the divine has chosen to get into the world through human beings. As a mentor of mine once said, this is the sort of story that *should* be true. And as Rachel Held Evans once said, "This is the story I will wrestle with for the rest of my life. This is the story I am willing to be wrong about."

Meister Eckhart once said that the virgin birth is something that happens within us, that the nativity story is the story of the continuing union of the Spirit of God with individual, fleshly human beings. But then Meister Eckhart was accused of heresy, was fortunate to escape being burned at the stake, and died in obscurity. No wonder his insight resonates with me. At the climactic manger scene in *The Nativity Story*, the gold-bearing wise man Melchior gazes at the baby and says, "God made into flesh." There it is in its simplicity and iconoclasm—the heart and soul of the Christian faith. God made into flesh.

"What's the difference between chili con carne and chili con queso?" I once asked my freshman students. "One is chili with meat, the other is chili with cheese," they replied, wanting to know why I would ask this stupid question with an obvious answer in the middle of a class on the Gospel of Luke. As I often do, I gave them a quick lesson in etymology (because, as I have told them many times, words are cool). "The Latin word 'carnis' means 'meat,'" I tell them. "It's where we get 'carnal,' 'carnivore,' 'carnage' and similar words from. Oh, and it's also the root of the word 'incarnation.'"

That grabs their attention. Although the students on my campus have become more diverse religiously, racially, and socioeconomically over the past several years, the majority of my students are still products of Catholic families and education, for whom the word "incarnation" is a sanitized church word used as a placeholder for the birth of Jesus. But what the doctrine of the Incarnation really means is something astounding and shocking. In becoming human, God chose to "become meat." And God still does.

"Incarnation" means "to put skin on." God's response to human need, hope, sorrow, desire, pain, joy, and suffering is to wrap the divine up in flesh. On a given day, in a given situation, that incarnated God might be you. It might be me. This is how the divine chooses to be in the world. It's much more possible to relate to someone with skin on than to a mathematical formula or a logical construct. God is not a Rubik's Cube. God is a person with skin on.

Instead of looking past the physical and ordinary for what is spiritual or profound, we might do well to remember that the most profound truth of Christianity is that God became flesh, became mundane, became embodied in the world that God created. And this incarnational activity continues in us. We are God's hands and feet—hands and feet that are made of meat. It may be that an increased focus on our carnality as God in the world is exactly what our age needs. Barbara Brown Taylor writes that

> [t]he last thing any of us needs is more information about God. We need the practice of incarnation, by which God saves the lives of those whose intellectual assent has turned as dry as dust, who have run frighteningly low on the bread of life, who are dying to know more God in their bodies.

I grew up in the same religious world that Barbara Brown Taylor comes from and, like her, was never told in church that my body is good, or that God takes delight in our bodies. But the resurrected Jesus had a body with the marks of death still on it, a body that could be prodded, poked, and still needed to be fed. A body that he took with him back to heaven. God trusted carnality to bring divine love into the world, and God still does. God decided a long time ago to trust human beings.

For reflection: Many traditional versions of Christianity teach that the body is spiritually problematic, yet the story of the Incarnation tells us that God chooses to get into the world through embodied, fleshly creatures. What might a fully embodied faith look like?

First Sunday After Christmas Day: "In the beginning was the Word"

Years A, B, C: John 1:1–18

The gospel reading in all three years for the First Sunday after Christmas is the familiar opening verses of John's gospel. These verses provide a beautifully poetic introduction to the greatest story ever told. Because the language is poetic rather than discursive, in these verses the author of John has provided two millennia of theologians and persons of faith with more to write, talk, pontificate, preach, argue, and be confused about than could possibly be exhausted in future millennia.

Logos, the word translated from the Greek as "Word," has many possible meanings, including "word," "thought," "principle," "speech," and "reason." That the author chose *logos* to begin the story opens the door to all sorts of possibilities . . . but not to the possibility that many Christians, including those in the evangelical Protestant world in which I grew up, insist upon. The first chapter of John makes it clear that the Word is not a text or a book, nor is it a collection of doctrines, dogmas, and traditions. The Word is a person.

I remember as if it were yesterday a conversation (debate? disagreement?) I had with someone on social media several years ago concerning the opening verses of John's gospel. In response to my suggestion that the Bible is a special book, but one written by human beings rather than dictated by God, the other person responded that anyone who denies the inerrancy of Scripture cannot legitimately call themselves "Christian." Rejecting scriptural inerrancy is the same as rejecting the authority of God in one's life.

I responded, rather defensively, that I found it sad to imagine a faith so narrow that it claims that God is confined within the covers of a book. That God somehow is incapable of speaking directly to contemporary human beings. That the Word of God is a book rather than a person. God is brought into the world through human beings, not ancient texts.

I could have done better. I could have used the very book that the fellow I was arguing with worships to make my point, as the next participant in the conversation did succinctly in short order by simply using John's gospel:

> *John 1:1—In the beginning was the Word. John 1:14—And the Word was made flesh and dwelt among us . . .*

The Bible isn't the Word of God, but it can lead us to the Word of God. The Word is not a book, in other words. The Word is a person.

In "An Essay on the Concept of Reading," Simone Weil reminds us that reading is more than deciphering words on a page:

> *There is a mystery in reading, a mystery which, if we contemplate it, may well help us, not to explain, but to grab hold of other mysteries in human life. . . . The sky, the seas, the sun, the stars, human beings, everything that surrounds us is something that we read.*

This insight includes a much broader understanding of "reading" than our traditional Western conception, which considers reading to be an exclusively cognitive, intellectual, and mental activity. Accordingly, I was grateful to discover a new kind of reading several years ago while on sabbatical.

I had heard about *lectio divina*, sacred reading, before I went on sabbatical to a Benedictine college campus with a large abbey on site, but it had not struck me as a particularly interesting concept. Just another skill to learn, technique to master, perhaps—but really, I thought, if there's one thing I know how to do pretty well, it's reading. After several weeks of daily prayer with the abbey monks, it dawned on me that *lectio divina* isn't about words, meaning, or retention at all. What was happening in the choir stalls was not a mind event, but a full-body experience bypassing my overdeveloped mind and seeping into all the other parts of me that had been starved for years: my bodily rhythms, my intuitions, my emotions, my spirit. The Psalms speak of God's word all the time, but almost never of thinking about God's word.

It's more like what Jeremiah reports: "Your words were found and I ate them, and your words became to me a joy and the delight of my heart." Simone Weil was channeling her internal Jeremiah when she wrote that "I only read what I am hungry for at the moment when I have an appetite for it, and then I do not read, I eat." And like a mother bird regurgitating food for its babies, an important word or phrase would come into my consciousness later in the day, one that I didn't remember reading but that had seeped into my soul.

In our "real world" of immediacy, getting it done, making money and a living, is there a place for what I began to absorb in a monastery abbey in middle-of-nowhere Minnesota? Over the subsequent years I've seen incremental but important evidence of change in how I converse with people, how I approach the day, and a heightened and more immediate sense of when a layer is threatening to grow back over my divine reading space.

Learning how to read differently is not just another technique; because it is a new way of being, it is transferable to everything. I went on sabbatical expecting to write about trying to sustain a life of faith when God at best is a silent partner who never writes, calls, emails, texts, or tweets. Now the divine is everywhere and seems to have a lot to say. Reading the divine begins with believing that everything is sacramental, infused with the breath of God, with taking "the Word became flesh" very seriously. All of creation is a sacred text. What are you reading?

For reflection: If the Word of God is a person rather than a book, consider the various ways in which people "read" each other. What are the tools we use to do this? How might these ways be appropriate for reading what is greater than us?

Second Sunday After Christmas Day: A different Christmas story

Year A: Matthew 2:13–23

The Year A text for Christmas 2 from Matthew's gospel is one of the most shocking stories in all of Scripture. The focus in the early chapters of Matthew is not on the birth of Jesus, but on events occurring soon after. "Wise men from the East" have arrived in Jerusalem after following a star that they believe portends the birth of a new king. After they refuse to take the current King Herod's bait and choose to return home after visiting the Holy Family's house (they had apparently moved out of the stable some time earlier) without revealing to Herod where the infant threat to his throne is living, Herod orders the murder of all the male children under two years of age in Bethlehem.

One of my favorite carols of the Christmas season is the Coventry Carol, so named because it is part of a cycle of sixteenth-century songs that were performed in that city as a dramatization of the birth narrative in Matthew. The music of the Coventry Carol is minor, appropriate for the shocking event that is its central concern:

Herod the king, in his raging,
Charged he hath this day.
His men of might, in his own sight,
All young children to slay.

Mary, Joseph, and Jesus escape the massacre because Joseph is tipped off by an angel of the danger. They travel to Egypt, where the family stays until Herod dies. The Coventry Carol reminds us that even the Incarnation, the divine taking on human form, does not guarantee a respite from darkness, evil, and death. Indeed, this particularly horrible event—the massacre of innocent children—would never have happened if not for the prior miraculous event of Jesus's birth. Again and again, we learn that goodness and evil exist together in a complex tangle that belies our hopes and dreams of a world in which all is goodness and light. Whatever is promised by the narrative of the Incarnation, it is not that.

The city of Coventry, after which the carol is named, was the location of yet another extraordinary mixture of hope and darkness during World War II. An industrial city in the West Midlands of England, Coventry was the target of numerous Luftwaffe bombing raids. The worst of these occurred on November 14, 1940; the devastation included the almost total destruction of Coventry's gothic Saint Michael's Cathedral, which was built during the late fourteenth and early fifteenth centuries.

Various researchers revealed some decades later that because the German secret "Enigma" code had just been broken by cryptographers at Bletchley Circle, British war authorities knew that Coventry had been targeted for a Luftwaffe fire-bombing raid some days before the raid occurred. These authorities chose not to alert the citizens of Coventry ahead of time because doing so would have revealed to the Germans that their supposedly unbreakable code had been cracked. Sir William Stephenson, the chief of all Allied intelligence during World War II, wrote that both Franklin Roosevelt and Winston Churchill were aware that Coventry was going to be bombed; Churchill reportedly told Stephenson after the war that letting Coventry burn aged him twenty years.

Others have challenged Stephenson's story, but stories of overall good joined with destruction and death are disturbingly commonplace. A new Coventry Cathedral was built next to the ruins of the one destroyed in 1940, incorporating into its modern architecture the remains of the previous edifice as a testament to both hope and despair, triumph and sacrifice.

The theme of the dedication, and the continuing ministry of St. Michael's Cathedral to this day, is reconciliation. Its artwork, commissioned from all over the world, makes use of remnants of the old cathedral as well as materials not usually incorporated in religious art—the wreckage of automobiles, refuse from landfills—the last places we normally look for intimations of the sacred.

Paying attention to the Christmas narrative reveals that the planners and parishioners of the cathedral in Coventry were on to something. When the divine enters the world, we may often look in vain for immediate evidence. Violence and suffering still occur, and human beings continue to perpetuate atrocities on each other and on the world in which we live. The difference before God enters human reality and after is so subtle it is often unnoticeable. But as a wise person once told me, this is not a God who intervenes. This is a God who indwells.

Anxiety and fear are natural human responses to evil and suffering. But we would do well to remember that one of the promised names of the infant to come—Immanuel—means "God is with us." We will unsuccessfully look far and wide for reminders of Herod's massacre of the innocents in nativity sets in houses and front yards during the Christmas season, but perhaps such reminders should be there. They are just as much a part of the story as angels singing to shepherds.

In the darkest depths of despair, the promise is that God is with us, choosing to become part of the mess and transform it from within rather than impose solutions from the outside. As I heard someone say recently, "We need to stop listening to fear and calling it wisdom." At the heart of the beautiful and transformative story is, as Winston Churchill might have described it, "a mystery wrapped in an enigma." A baby in a manger, as well as the dead babies in the streets of Bethlehem, call us to embrace hope when things are darkest. We are not alone.

For reflection: A frequent question asked when something tragic or destructive happens is "How could God have let this happen?" How might the story of God's becoming human, embedded in the midst of a world that contains evil and suffering, frame possible answers to this difficult question?

Second Sunday After Christmas Day: Jesus goes about His Father's business

Year C: Luke 2:41–52

The Christmas 2 Year C gospel reading from Luke 2 provides us with a rare glimpse into Holy Family dynamics. Lots of people think their children are special. Everyone thinks their child is precocious and the smartest/best looking/most creative human being ever. Every parent expects their infant to earn either a full academic or full athletic scholarship (probably both) to the college of their choice when the time comes.

In *The Nativity Story*, a significant amount of time is spent on Mary and Joseph's journey from Nazareth south to Bethlehem in obedience to Caesar's census command. The filmmaker creatively lets us spend some time with these two young people, almost strangers to each other, who have been named as players in a divine plan about which they have been told very little. At one point, Mary asks Joseph what the angel had said to him.

> **Joseph**: He said to not be afraid. (pause) Are you afraid?
> **Mary**: Yes. Are you?
> **Joseph**: Yes.
> **Mary**: Do you ever wonder when we'll know? That he is not just a child? Something he says, a look in his eyes?
> **Joseph**: Sometimes I wonder will I be able to even teach him anything.

No kidding. When an angel tells Joseph in a dream that the soon-to-be-born baby will "save his people from their sins," one's possible parental and step-parental contributions pale in comparison.

A baby born on a bed of straw and dung to parents who are just as clueless about what to do next as any first-time parents would be. Who will this baby grow up to be? When did it become clear that something unusual was going on with this kid? Søren Kierkegaard wrote that life is easy to understand looking backward (or at least we think it is), but we often forget that life has to be lived forward. It's worth trying to approach the Nativity and its accompanying stories forward, starting from the beginning, instead of looking back already claiming to know the answers.

Although you wouldn't know it from the mass quantities of commentary and artwork that have been produced over the last two thousand years, the canonical Gospels tell us remarkably little about Holy Family life. They essentially leave us in the dark about Jesus between birth and thirty years old. We get the circumcision, the three kings, the flight to Egypt, Jesus growing in wisdom and stature, and the reading from Luke, twelve-year-old Jesus in the temple. The various artist's renditions I've seen of this story are pretty much the same—Jesus, in the center of a holy glow, pontificates and astounds while his learned elders in the shadows lean away in disbelief and awe and some scribe takes notes.

The actual story gives us a glimpse into a real family, holy or not. After going to the feast in Jerusalem with friends and family, as is their annual custom, Mary and Joseph head back north to Nazareth. Although they're not sure where Jesus is, they assume that he's running around with his friends somewhere in the traveling group, so they don't worry about it. Good for them—he's almost a teenager, and they've loosened the parental leash a little bit. Let the kid have some freedom.

But when he doesn't show up at the end of the day, they're worried. After failing to find him in the caravan, they return in a panic to Jerusalem, where after three days they find him in the temple "sitting in the midst of the teachers." In response to his mother's exasperated and relieved, "*What the hell is your problem?? We've been looking all over for you!!! We thought you'd been kidnapped!!!!*" Jesus gives a predictable, smart-alecky twelve-year-old response: "Why is it that you sought me? Did you not know that I must be about my Father's business?" Oh, really? "Guess what? You're grounded! Once we get back to Nazareth you can 'be about your Father's business' *in your room!!*" Luke chooses not to tell us if Jesus lived under house arrest for the next year.

This is a real family, struggling with the challenges of love, faith, boundaries, and growing up. Despite the usual interpretations of this story, I think that Jesus did not go to the Temple to school the experts—something he presumably could have done, given his pedigree. He was "sitting in the midst of the teachers, both listening to them and asking them questions."

I don't know whether twelve-year-old Jesus thought he was the Son of God—my guess is that he didn't. But he did know where he wanted to be—he wanted to be where he could learn. Certainly the mystery and splendor of the Temple would have been an attraction for any young Jewish boy. But the real attraction was that this is where learning happened. This is where the most intelligent and educated people of Jesus's society gathered to debate, to investigate, to discuss, and to discover. And that's where Jesus wanted to be—listening and asking questions. Even the Son of God had a lot to learn and knew how to get started: Put yourself in the right place and open yourself up.

The life of learning is far more about quietness, attentive listening, and perceptive questions than conveying facts and information. This is where the divine in each of our human vessels gets awakened and fanned into flame. It's a privilege to participate. When, as always happens, I find myself buried under and frustrated by piles of grading and endless department and committee meetings, I try to remember twelve-year-old Jesus, who knew where he belonged. He was about his Father's business. Go and do likewise.

For reflection: The story of Jesus in the temple reports that he was "listening . . . and asking questions." To what extent is the life of faith more about listening and questioning than about answers and certainty?

CHAPTER 3

Epiphany—Jesus's Coming Out Party

The season of Epiphany always begins on January 6 (after the twelve days of Christmas), but the season is of variable length. Epiphany ends at Ash Wednesday, the beginning of Lent; because Ash Wednesday comes forty-six days before Easter and the date of Easter is variable depending on things like full moons and the spring equinox, the end of Epiphany can be anytime between the beginning of February and the middle of March. The season of Epiphany can have as few as four or as many as nine Sundays.

Epiphany is one of the liturgical seasons (the others are Advent and Lent) that was news to me when I first encountered it. "Epiphany" etymologically means "manifestation" or "to show forth"; the season celebrates the first revealing of Christ to the Gentiles through the visit of the Magi, marked on January 6. In other words, Epiphany celebrates Jesus's coming out party. As we will see, several of the most familiar events and miracles in Jesus's early ministry are central texts in the Epiphany lectionary readings.

Epiphany of the Lord

Years A, B, C: Matthew 2:1–12

The gospel reading in all three years for Epiphany is the familiar story from Matthew 2 where wise men from the East, following a star, end up at the house where Jesus, Mary, and Joseph live. For a number of reasons, Epiphany has come to be very meaningful to me over the years, beginning with an unexpected epiphany on a Sunday morning bus trip to church that began with overhearing a public conversation.

> *It's the cold mornings that are the hardest. You want nothing more than to wake up in your own place, look out the window, make some coffee, and not have to go anywhere.*
>
> *They've given me ten days. Who the hell can find a place to live in ten days? The only place you can find in the winter in ten days is an abandoned building.*
>
> *But I'll sleep anywhere instead of going to a shelter. Some of the people in shelters are nasty. No matter how hard you try to mind your own business, somebody just has to get in your face and then it's on.*
>
> *You're telling me. A lot of those people never take showers, not that I blame them because the shelter bathrooms are disgusting. Animals wouldn't want to use them.*
>
> *I sat too close to someone's backpack one time, and he kicked me.*

Not the sort of conversation I usually hear on a Sunday morning. But then I don't usually ride the bus to church. "It'll be fun," I thought to myself. "It will be an adventure." Jeanne had the car in New Jersey for a work commitment, and I felt like going to church. I spent a half-hour on the public transportation website the night before, eventually calculating that it actually was possible to get there from here, but just barely.

As I waited for my bus downtown, I looked inside the terminal. It was crowded with at least one hundred people of various sizes, shapes, ages, and races. Most were dressed in some sort of winter garb, designer or makeshift; I guessed that half of them weren't even waiting for a bus. A few minutes later as I boarded the bus that would take me ten miles south to church, two gentlemen—a thirty-something and a guy ten years or so older—got on and sat across the aisle.

Before long they started talking about how difficult they found it to preserve a shred of dignity while being homeless. As I eavesdropped on their conversation, I was grateful for my good fortune and blessings and silently asked God to bless them. *Please help our elected officials to figure something out. You are a God of love and justice, and these men need a lot of both. Amen*—and they got off the bus, leaving me to travel the remaining ten minutes to church in silence.

Since the Feast of the Epiphany happened to fall on Sunday that year, the day's texts from the Jewish Scriptures were from Epiphany 1, Year A. Psalm 29 says that "the voice of the LORD flashes forth flames of fire . . . the voice of the LORD causes the oaks to whirl and strips the forest bare; and in his temple all say, 'Glory!'" Now that's what I'm talking about! That's a God who can straighten things out and bring on justice like a flood. Enough with our puny human attempts! But Isaiah says something very different about the one who is to come, the one who "will bring forth justice to the nations."

> *He will not cry or lift up his voice or make it heard in the street; a bruised reed he will not break, and a dimly burning wick he will not quench; he will faithfully bring forth justice.*

How is someone so gentle that he won't break a bruised reed or snuff out an almost spent candle going to bring about justice?

Then it dawns on me—a little epiphany, I suppose—that I encountered the bruised reeds and dimly burning wicks of our day and age sitting across from me on the way to church. These were the people I read about in the paper and hear the talking heads screech about on 24/7 news channels, but with real faces and living real histories. These guys actually existed, not as specimens from the social category labeled "homeless," but as men, exactly like me, who were one day stamped with a special mark by affliction and misfortune.

How to respond? I might begin just by paying attention. Simone Weil writes that

> [t]hose who are unhappy have no need for anything but people capable of giving them their attention . . . The soul empties itself of all its own contents in order to receive into itself the being it is looking at, just as he is, in all his truth.

In other words, before I try to solve your problem, tell me your story. Justice for bruised reeds and almost-extinguished wicks must begin in peace, gentleness, and silent attentiveness. Various sorts of force have just about finished them off. Any more might be the end.

But who on earth could do this? Isaiah's answer is disturbingly direct:

> I am the LORD, I have called you in righteousness . . . I have given you as a covenant to the people, a light to the nations, to open the eyes that are blind, to bring out the prisoners from the dungeon, from the prison those who sit in darkness . . . See, the former things have come to pass, and new things I now declare; before they spring forth, I tell you of them.

Epiphany basks in the glorious light of the Incarnation, of the divine made flesh. And nowadays that's me. That's you. That's us. Only from that very unpromising source will justice roll down like waters, and righteousness as a mighty stream.

For reflection: Where are the "bruised reeds" in your life? What would it be like to listen to and hear their stories before trying to "fix" them or "solve" their problems?

First Sunday After Epiphany: The baptism of Jesus

Year A: Matthew 3:13–17; Year B: Mark 1:7–11; Year C: Luke 3:15–16, 21–22

The gospel reading for Epiphany 1 is Jesus's baptism by John the Baptist; the versions in the Synoptic Gospels are remarkably similar. This gets me thinking about the different ways in which the Christian groups I have spent my life with have handled baptism. What is the proper way to do it? Why do it at all? This takes me back more than four decades . . .

What is the best way to get the attention of a bunch of Episcopalians? I learned the answer to this question when, after my first Sunday morning Episcopal worship service, I found myself downstairs in what they called the "undercroft" for coffee hour. There were at least fifty people gathered, eating pastries, drinking coffee, some smoking cigarettes (of all things); the noise of conversation was deafening. Then the dean of the cathedral entered the room and loudly said, "***THE LORD BE WITH YOU!***" Upon which everyone parroted back, "***AND ALSO WITH YOU!***"

This phrase introduces important chunks of liturgy every week, including the baptism of a baby, an event that I experienced for the first time soon after I started attending Episcopal services. Baptizing infants was one of the few things that gave me pause when I was new to the Episcopal Church. So much about the Episcopal way of doing things was attractive and an obvious spiritual balm to the scars I carried from my conservative, fundamentalist upbringing. Liturgy, a pipe organ, excellent music, clerical robes, a prayer book, weekly (even daily)

Eucharist—if I had been aware enough to design worship that spoke to my deepest aesthetic and spiritual needs, it would have been exactly like Sunday morning at St. Matthew's Cathedral.

But this baby-baptizing business was weird. After finishing the baptismal liturgy, the dean would carry the baby up and down the center aisle of the cathedral, saying, "This is the brand-newest Christian in the world!" as the congregation applauded. For someone taught from his earliest memory that becoming a Christian demanded a "born-again experience," a once-and-for-all conversion event that required a certain level of rational maturity and spiritual awareness, this business of becoming a Christian simply by some water being poured on one's head in the manner specified by the prayer book was jarring.

My own full-immersion baptism, performed by my father in a baptismal font the size of a small swimming pool when I was twelve, was what a baptism is supposed to be like. I've always thought, despite sacred art and Hollywood depictions, that John the Baptist did not just pour a bit of water on Jesus's head that day in the Jordan River—he dunked him. Several decades later, I find it somewhat amusing and quaint that I thought baby-baptizing might be a deal breaker. There are a few essentials in the Christian faith—the Incarnation, for instance—but the proper method to baptize someone, let alone the meaning of baptism, probably is not one of them.

The longer I commit to following Jesus, the more I resist attempts to nail down the essentials. Try systematizing the mystery of the Trinity and see how far you get before losing the mystery entirely. The beautiful words toward the end of the Episcopal baptismal liturgy point toward another mystery—"You are marked as Christ's own forever." If I believe that to be true, then former doctrinal issues with baptizing children dissolve into irrelevance.

In Iris Murdoch's novel *Nuns and Soldiers*, a central character has a vision in which she is visited in her kitchen by Jesus. As he leaves the room after a brief conversation, Jesus touches the woman on the hand. After the vision ends, she knows that her experience was not simply imaginary, because her hand is painfully burned where Jesus touched her. Although the burn heals, and the pain eventually fades over the following days, a small but permanent scar remains. For the rest of her life the scar is an indelible reminder that she is forever changed because one day she encountered Jesus.

Perhaps baptism is something like that. Somewhere in the past and continuing history of those who are scarred by the mark of Christ are events, people, decisions, and experiences that form the skeleton, the internal structure of faith. A person's spiritual identity is shaped by this structure, fleshed out in ways unique to each individual.

Some pieces of this identity come out of the blue, divinely tinged experiences that cannot be easily accommodated or dismissed. Others are deliberately chosen, such as a baptism, responding to an altar call, a choice of worship community, or turning away from what no longer gives life. As a person baptized as an infant grows older, that person will be able to identify their baptismal Sunday as a signpost of difference, even though they did not choose that signpost themselves. The imprint of the divine on a human life often has nothing to do with individual choice. The Lord be with you . . . as the Lord always is.

For reflection: What does baptism mean to you? What role does your own baptism play in your understanding of your unique spiritual journey?

Second Sunday After Epiphany: The wedding at Cana

Year C: John 2:1–11

The Epiphany 2 Year C reading from John's gospel is the wedding feast at Cana, the only gospel in which Jesus's miracle of turning water into wine is recorded. It often is helpful to reimagine the gospel stories, including the miracles, as just another day in the lives of people two thousand years ago who were, undoubtedly, as clueless about the big picture as we tend to be in our own contemporary lives. The wedding at Cana is Jesus's first public miracle.

My father was a conservative Protestant minister; accordingly, I was raised in a world in which alcoholic beverages were forbidden. But my father was also evolving in his faith journey as I grew from childhood into adolescence. Imagine my shock when I returned from school one day and discovered my father sitting in our living room, reading the Bible, listening to classical music, and drinking a glass of . . . wine.

Even in his most buttoned-down Baptist days, my father was an iconoclast. He delighted in saying things from the pulpit intended to disturb and even shock those who were comfortable in their dogmatic certainty about all things God-related. He would ask things like, "What are we supposed to make of a guy who made vats of the best wine anyone had ever tasted for his first miracle?" Good question.

All of the characters in *The Chosen*, an ongoing cinematic treatment of the life of Jesus, are treated as real persons with recognizable human strengths, weaknesses, and peccadilloes—Jesus included. The centerpiece of the fifth episode in season one is the wedding at Cana. Jesus's mother Mary is best friends with Dinah, the mother of the groom, and arrives early to help with preparations for the wedding ceremony and celebration that evening.

As the day progresses, Mary keeps her eye out for her son, Jesus, who is on the invitation list and is expected to attend the wedding. As she and Dinah discuss Jesus, whom she clearly loves but does not fully understand, Mary mentions to Dinah that "a few" extra people may be coming with Jesus, a motley and ever-growing group of people attracted to the charismatic young rabbi. Dinah generously says that everyone is welcome but secretly knows that adding in even a few extra people will undoubtedly put a strain on the food and drink budget and supply already stretched to the limit.

Eventually, Jesus arrives with Simon, Andrew, James, John, Nathaniel, Thaddeus, another James ("little James" in contrast to "big James" who is a head taller), and Mary Magdalene, people whose backstories have been developing over the earlier episodes. Other unexpected and uninvited folks also show up, making the actual number of attendees twice as large as had been planned for. When this is announced to Thomas and Ramah, the caterers in charge of food and drink, it becomes clear what a huge problem this is. The party is expected to go on for days, everyone expects to be drinking a great deal of wine, and the wine purchased for the event is already gone.

You know what happens next. Mary pulls Jesus, who is having a great time with his friends dancing and telling stories, aside and asks him to do something about the problem, which, if unaddressed, will be devastatingly embarrassing for her friend Dinah and her husband. In the gospel account, Jesus is rude to his mother, saying, "Woman, what concern is that to you and to me? My hour has not yet come."

In *The Chosen*, Jesus is fortunately less of a jerk and, upon hearing about the wine shortage, asks, "Why are you telling me this? My time has not yet come," perhaps unsure even himself about his own capacities and abilities. In an inspired response that is not in the gospel, Mary replies, "If not now, when?" Jesus nods and proceeds over the next few minutes to turn water in large stone containers into the best wine anyone present has ever tasted.

The only people who know that a miracle has occurred are Jesus, his mother, Thomas, and Ramah. Thomas, who has showed himself throughout the episode to be a no-nonsense, logical, numbers sort of guy, tells Ramah at the end of the episode that Jesus has invited him to join his growing entourage in Samaria twelve days later. When Ramah asks whether he is going to do it, Thomas says, "I don't know what to think." Ramah, who knows Thomas well (and suspects that he has a thing for her), replies, "So don't. Maybe for once in your life, don't think."

When it comes to the reported miracles of Jesus, this is excellent advice. Earlier in the episode, when it becomes clear what has happened, Ramah asks, "Who is he? I can't pretend I didn't see a miracle." For me, and I suspect for many of us who call ourselves Christian, this line captures why I am a person of faith. Miracles come in all shapes and sizes, both unmistakable and inexplicable. Anne Lamott writes that "Grace means you're in a different universe from where you had been stuck, when you had absolutely no way to get there on your own." That's a miracle. Faith is committing yourself to seeing how that miracle plays out.

For reflection: Simone Weil writes that "the stories of miracles complicate everything." Do you agree? How important to your relationship with Jesus are the stories of his miracles? And why did he regularly tell those who witnessed his miracles not to tell anyone?

Third Sunday After Epiphany: "Today . . . in your hearing"

Year C: Psalm 19; Luke 4:14–21

"Faith and Doubt" is a team-taught colloquium I teach with a colleague from the political science department who is also a Dominican priest. We begin the semester with Anne Lamott's *Plan B*; her observation that "the opposite of faith is not doubt, but certainty—certainty is missing the point entirely" serves as our starting point.

Lamott's orientation to faith and related matters is established early in *Plan B* when she quotes Henri Matisse, who said that "I don't know if I believe in God or not ... But the essential thing is to put oneself in a frame of mind which is close to that of prayer." Prayer has little to do with the content of one's beliefs and everything to do with orientation and attitude. A "prayerful" attitude is an example of what Simone Weil calls "attentiveness," a deliberate openness to everything that isn't me and a willingness to remove the filters of the ego as I look.

Psalm 19, the Year C lectionary psalm for Epiphany 3, invites us to turn our attention upward and outward toward the wonders of creation, which, without words or sound, communicates more than could be processed in a lifetime.

> *The heavens are telling the glory of God; and the firmament proclaims his handiwork.*
> *Day to day pours forth speech, and night to night declares knowledge.*
> *There is no speech, nor are there words; their voice is not heard;*
> *yet their voice goes out through all the earth, and their words to the end of the world.*

Lamott places prayer in the space that the psalmist is celebrating when she writes that "[w]hen you pray, you are not starting the conversation from scratch, just remembering to plug back into a conversation that's always in progress."

The beginning of Psalm 19 is so powerful that it is easy to forget the many beautiful verses throughout. I particularly love the final verse:

> *Let the words of my mouth and the meditation of my heart,*
> *be acceptable to you, O Lord, my rock and my redeemer.*

I have this prayer in mind at the beginning of every class that I teach. It's good to be reminded that there's a lot more going on here than just me.

The Year C gospel reading for Epiphany 3 is the story from Luke's gospel in which a bunch of people in a Nazareth synagogue find out that there's a lot more going on than they thought. Jesus is fresh off his forty days and nights of temptation in the desert and returns to Nazareth, his hometown. What better place to kick off his ministry?

The scene is powerfully portrayed in the 1977 Franco Zeffirelli television mini-series *Jesus of Nazareth*. It is the Sabbath, and Jesus is in the synagogue with wall-to-wall men and boys, while the women of the town observe from behind a screen. Although it is apparently not his turn to read, Jesus steps to the front and takes the scroll. After a pregnant pause, he begins to read from Isaiah 61:

> *The Spirit of the Lord is upon me*
> *because he has anointed me to bring good news to the poor.*
> *He has sent me to proclaim release to the captives*
> *and recovery of sight to the blind,*
> *to let the oppressed go free,*
> *to proclaim the year of the Lord's favor.*

When he is finished, Jesus rolls up the scroll, makes eye contact with the congregation, and says, "Today, this scripture has been fulfilled in your hearing."

As the camera slowly pans the faces of those at the synagogue, their expressions pass from piety, to confusion, to outrage and anger. For every man and woman present knows that this scripture can only be fulfilled by the Messiah. And they know who *this* man is. He is Mary and Joseph's son. He is a carpenter—a bit odd at times, but the same as they are. "I remember when I chased you out of my bakery for stealing a fig," one thinks. "I remember when I had to break up a squabble between you and my son when you were teenagers," thinks another. And he has just declared himself to be the Messiah. No wonder they tried to kill him.

Christians believe that, despite the appropriate incredulity of his fellow worshippers on that Sabbath, Jesus was indeed the Messiah, God in flesh. But even more remarkable is that these 2,500-year-old words from Isaiah were not only fulfilled by Jesus—they continue to be fulfilled by God in human form. Isaiah's prophecy foretells a time when healing, justice, and liberation will be brought to the sick, oppressed, and prisoners.

That time is *now*, and *we* are the vehicles of that healing, justice, and liberation. Our world is full of the poor, the bound, those who mourn, those who are in captivity both physically and mentally. We live in a world crying out for liberation, peace, and consolation at every level. So often we wonder where God is, where the divine solution to the never-ending problems and tragedies of our world is to be found.

But we miss the clear answer to our questions. Joan Chittister writes that

> [h]aving made the world, having given it everything it needs to continue, having brought it to the point of abundance and possibility and dynamism, God left it for us to finish. God left it to us to be the mercy and the justice, the charity and the care, the righteousness, and the commitment, all that it will take for people to bring the goodness of God to outweigh the rest.

We are to be the oil of joy for those who mourn, to be the beauty in the midst of ashes, and to wrap the heavy of heart in the garment of praise. As the closing prayer in each Eucharistic celebration in the Episcopal liturgy asks, "[S]end us now into the world in peace, and grant us strength and courage to love and serve you with gladness and singleness of heart."

For reflection: If you had been present at the Nazareth synagogue when Jesus said that he was the fulfillment of Isaiah's prophecy, how would you have reacted?

Fourth Sunday After Epiphany: "Blessed are . . ."

Year A: Matthew 5:1–12

Epiphany 4 Year A is the first of five Sundays whose gospel readings focus on the Sermon on the Mount in Matthew's gospel. It is a scene so familiar in our imaginations that it has become iconic. On the top of a hill in the middle of the impromptu gathering is the man everybody has been talking about and has gathered to check out. He doesn't look any different from any number of other guys in the crowd. In spite of the stories that seem to pop up everywhere this man goes, you would not be able to pick him out of a lineup. Then he opens his mouth, and the world is forever changed. Here is Matthew's full version of the Beatitudes:

> *Blessed are the poor in spirit, for theirs is the kingdom of heaven.*
> *Blessed are those who mourn, for they will be comforted.*
> *Blessed are the meek, for they will inherit the earth.*
> *Blessed are those who hunger and thirst for righteousness, for they will be filled.*
> *Blessed are the merciful, for they will receive mercy.*
> *Blessed are the pure in heart, for they will see God.*
> *Blessed are the peacemakers, for they will be called children of God.*
> *Blessed are those who are persecuted for righteousness' sake, for theirs is the kingdom of heaven.*
> *Blessed are you when people revile you and persecute you and utter all kinds of evil against you falsely on my account.*

Rejoice and be glad, for your reward is great in heaven.

We don't know the details of the setting, of course—the traditional images are evocations of centuries of imagination. Maybe it was a cloudy and windy day. Maybe these words were spoken inside someone's home or a synagogue. Maybe they were shared in private only with a few intimate friends and confidants. Maybe the man never spoke these words at all and they are intended as a brief summary, written decades after the fact, of how he lived and called others to live.

But the Beatitudes are so beautifully poetic, so rich yet sparse, so gentle yet powerful, so all-encompassing and embracing that over the centuries they have seeped into the Christian ethos as the summary expression, as the "mission statement" of a religion and all it professes to stand for. The beauty and familiarity of the language can easily disguise what is most remarkable about the Beatitudes—they are a crystal clear call to radically uproot everything we think we know about value, about what is important, about prestige, about power, and even about God. They are a challenge to fundamentally change the world.

The Roman-dominated world into which these words came like a lightning bolt was not that different from our own. One's status or rank in the social hierarchy depended on factors such as power, birth, economic status, education, gender, race—usually some combination of these. Those who lacked these qualities, whether through their own fault or because of matters entirely outside their control, had little opportunity to rise above their lowly state.

In a matter of a few brief, poetic lines Jesus turns it all upside-down. In God's economy, *none* of our assumptions can be relied upon and none of our commonsense arrangements work. God's values are apparently the very opposite of those produced by our natural human wiring. Throughout the rest of the Sermon on the Mount, and consistently throughout virtually everything we have that is attributed to Jesus in the Gospels, the point is driven home. God is most directly found in the poor, the widows, the orphans, the disenfranchised, all those for whom pretensions of being something or having influence are unavailable.

The Gospels are clear that the one thing guaranteed to make God angry is to ignore such persons. The infrequent times that Jesus talks about hell are always in the context of people who spend their lives ignoring the unfortunate. Because in truth we *all* are impoverished, we *all* are abandoned, we *all* are incapable of taking care of ourselves, let alone of anyone else. The poor, widows, and orphans simply no longer have the luxury of pretending otherwise.

Every once in a while we hear on the news or read online about a community in which a debate has arisen over whether it is permissible to put a plaque or a statue containing the Ten Commandments in a law court, a state house, or a public school. But imagine a community or a society with governing practices and policies infused with the energy, not of the Ten Commandments, but of the Beatitudes. Imagine a legislative body whose guiding North Star was the mercy and compassion of the Beatitudes rather than the cold and clinical justice of the Ten Commandments. How would such a community's or society's attitudes and policies concerning the poor, the disenfranchised, those who are struggling, those who have fallen through the cracks, change as it learned to see such "unfortunates" not as a problem, but rather as the very face of God?

An intriguing thought experiment, but ultimately the Beatitudes are not about transformed social institutions. They are about a transformational way of being in the world. The Beatitudes are far more than a beautifully poetic literary statement. They are the road map for how to carry faith into the real world. The world we live in is no more naturally attuned to the challenge of the Beatitudes than was the world in which they were first spoken. Individuals infected with the energy of the

Beatitudes are those whose responsibility it is to help transform reality. The Beatitudes are a call to get to work.

For reflection: Imagine that you were present at the Sermon on the Mount. How would the Beatitudes have struck you if you were a wealthy person? A person with political or religious authority? A person accustomed to looking away from those most in need?

Fifth Sunday After Epiphany: "The light of the world"

Year A: Matthew 5:13–14

The gospel reading for Epiphany 5 Year A continues with the Sermon on the Mount. Immediately after the Beatitudes, Jesus tells his audience that they are "the salt of the earth" and "the light of the world." Light is a central and important theme throughout the Gospels; we will have the opportunity to explore the metaphor as we proceed through the liturgical year.

Shortly before the 2013 conclave that would elect him as Pope Francis I, Cardinal Jorge Mario Bergoglio urged his fellow cardinals to remember that Christians should live by the light of the moon rather than that of the sun. Followers of Christ should reflect the source of light rather than acting as if they are the source. With regard to the hierarchy of the religious structure he would soon be elected to lead, he said that the Church exists to reflect Christ—as soon as it believes it is itself the light, disaster occurs and the Church becomes an idol.

Francis's insight reminds me of a distinction that Barbara Brown Taylor makes between "solar" and "lunar" spirituality. Solar spirituality, on the one hand, emphasizes the sunny side of faith, including confidence in God's presence, certainty of belief, divine guidance in all things, and reliable answers to prayer. For those gifted with lunar spirituality, on the other hand, the life of faith is not the same from day to day—there are times of light and times of darkness.

Although I am by nature more lunar than solar, Taylor's categories are about far more than personality types, and Pope Francis's distinction between the sun and the moon in understanding the Church has deep implications for the life of faith. Almost every important belief and activity in the spiritual realm looks different when viewed from a lunar rather than a solar perspective.

Consider prayer, for instance. I grew up in a fully solar religious world where prayers were offered positively, consistently, loudly, and in expectation of regular and reliable answers. We loved hearing and talking about stories of answered prayer from Scripture and our own experience, celebrating the many ways in which God responded to our prayers. The measure of a prayer's effectiveness was whether it was answered. Midweek prayer services were filled with testimonies of "what the Lord has done for me" during the past week. The fact that our fervent prayers often went unanswered and the presence of the divine was often undetectable didn't matter—we were urged to live out a religious version of "fake it 'til you make it" because, after all, how can you not be happy when God is on your side?

Prayer according to the solar model is energized by the person doing the praying. We called people who appeared to be particularly successful at attracting God's attention "prayer warriors," an unfortunate turn of phrase because from it and similar phrases I learned early on that the spiritual life is a struggle, involving warfare and all of the characteristics that define a good soldier. A prayer warrior, it seemed to me, was someone who could pray for longer periods of time and more loudly than others, but one earned this title only if a few, or even one, of one's prayers had identifiably been answered at some point.

The solar model of prayer is transactional. "I'll do this for you and you do this for me." This conception of a prayer-answering God has a solid pedigree—the Bible contains many passages in which God clearly invites the believer to ask for things, to express her heart's desire, to "call to me and I will answer you." But there comes a time in the life of any person of faith when the silence from the other end of the transaction becomes deafening.

This is where thinking about prayer as lunar rather than solar is helpful. A useful question to ask is: "What if prayer is something *that you are* rather than something *that you do*?" In the solar model, prayer is an activity generated by the person praying in hopes that the activity is being done with the energy and content that the divine approves of. But as Pope Francis told his fellow cardinals, it is a mistake in the life of faith to consider oneself as the energy source.

If prayer is lunar rather than solar, then prayer becomes a matter of reflecting the divine light into the world in whatever way that light is shining on you and in you at the time. It is not up to me to generate the light; rather, it is up to me to reflect divine reality in ways that are unique to me and represent the seasons and cycles of my life. This is the point of Paul's directive in 1 Thessalonians to "pray without ceasing." No one can pray all of the time, but each of us can become a prayer as we continue to become the person that God intends us to be. Prayer becomes a matter of becoming a certain sort of person, rather than becoming better and better at doing certain kinds of things.

It is not up to us to draw God's attention through perfected prayer performance art—God is already here. Rather, we are to reflect the light of the divine uniquely as incarnated beings who bear that light within us. Becoming a prayer is undoubtedly a lifelong process, but there is no better place to start than with the advice Paul provides to the church at Philippi. "Finally, whatever things are true ... honest ... just ... pure ... lovely ... of good report. If there is any virtue, if there is any praise, think on these things." As we consider these things, we begin to reflect them as we become mirrors of the divine light. We begin to be a prayer.

For reflection: Is your faith more solar or lunar? Do you find that your answer depends on circumstances? What difference is there between "being" light and "reflecting" light?

Sixth Sunday After Epiphany: "You can make me clean"

Year B: 2 Kings 5:1–14; Mark 1:40–45

While the Year A and C gospel readings for Epiphany 6 continue with portions of the Sermon on the Mount, the Year B gospel is Mark's account of Jesus healing a leper who comes to Jesus saying, "If you choose, you can make me clean." Mark's gospel is the earliest and briefest of the Gospels, focusing far more on what Jesus does than what Jesus says. In typical fashion, Mark's Jesus in response to the leper says, "I do choose. Be made clean!" and the leper is healed.

The reading from the Jewish Scriptures for the day involves another leper who is miraculously healed. The story of Naaman in 2 Kings 5 contains many powerful lessons that remain relevant thousands of years later, including some important truths about faith, human nature, and class distinctions. Along the way, it also shows how important it is to listen to the people in your life, even those whom you doubt have anything important to say.

Naaman was a powerful and important man, the head general of the armies of the king of Syria to the north of the kingdom of Israel. Naaman was "a mighty warrior," but he also suffered from leprosy. In Naaman's household was a young Israelite girl whom he had taken captive in a raid across the border and who now was servant to Naaman's wife. Upon hearing of her master's affliction, the servant girl tells Naaman's wife of a man in Israel, the prophet Elisha, who would be able to heal Naaman if her master would travel to Samaria, the capital of Israel, where Elisha was often to be found.

This sets in motion a great tale of crossed wires, politics gone awry, delusions of grandeur exposed, and humility leading to healing. Naaman gets the king of Syria to contact the king of Israel and set in motion the diplomatic process needed to facilitate Naaman's journey to Samaria. The king of Israel assumes that the official story is "fake news," suspecting that a trap is being set. An important man from Syria is coming to Samaria, expecting to be healed. The king of Israel has no healing skills, and the ensuing failure will be taken by the king of Syria as an insult. The news puts the king of Israel in a panic; word of the situation filters out to Elisha, and Elisha sends word to the king that he should simply send Naaman Elisha's way, and everything will be fine. "Please let him come to me," Elisha says, "and he shall know that there is a prophet in Israel."

Upon his arrival at Elisha's house, Naaman is ready to let the healing begin, prepared to perform any number of feats appropriate for an important person in order to receive a cure. But instead of coming out to meet Naaman, Elisha simply sends word that Naaman should head for the muddy Jordan River down the road, wash in it seven times, and he will be cured of his leprosy. Naaman is insulted. "Doesn't this guy know who he's dealing with? I'm an important man—at least he could meet me in person and say some magic words! And if all it takes is washing in a river, I could have done that in one of our far superior rivers back in Syria!" And he departs in a huff.

Fortunately, Naaman's servants know what to do when the master gets upset. Give him some space, let him cool down, then speak to him calmly. "If the prophet had asked you to do something great, would you not have done it?" they ask Naaman. "Of course you would have—so why become angry over doing something as simple as washing in the river? What do you have to lose? Do it and see what happens!" Naaman listens to reason, washes seven times in the Jordan, and his leprosy is cured. Problem solved, and everyone goes home happy.

The overall point of the story in the Jewish Scriptures has to do with the greatness of Yahweh, that divine healing and mercy are available to all regardless of their ethnicity or social status, and how divine plans are just about never what we might predict. But there is an additional message here that sometimes gets missed, one that people in power—past, present, and future—would do well to learn.

Notice who the heroes of this story are. Not Naaman. Not even Elisha the prophet. The heroes are nameless nobodies, people whose gender and/or social status made them invisible on a daily basis. First, a young woman from Israel who is Naaman's slave has the temerity to offer an opinion to her mistress, Naaman's wife. "I think I know how master Naaman can be helped," she says. Both her mistress and the master himself listen and act accordingly. Later, Naaman's servants know how to handle their master and get him to do what needs to be done, when they could have simply said "not my problem" as Naaman raged.

The takeaway? Listen to the insights and ideas of those around you, even if you are convinced that you are better than they are. Even if you think you know more than everyone else. Even if everyone in your life is continually pointing out just how fabulous you are. Chances are that you don't know everything, even if you are the commander of a large army. Even if you are the most powerful person in the world. Naaman's primary virtue is that he was able to receive advice and input even from those who, by societal standards, were not his "equals," and was willing to act on that advice. This virtue is currently in short supply.

For reflection: The Scriptures are full of stories in which God speaks profoundly through the least likely voices. Who are the "invisible" people in your life, the ones whom you barely notice but who might just have wisdom to offer?

Seventh Sunday After Epiphany: "Be perfect"

Year A: Matthew 5:38–48; Luke 6:27–38

As they continue through the Sermon on the Mount, Epiphany 7 gospel texts present a seemingly impossible challenge. "Be perfect. . as your heavenly Father is perfect," Jesus says in Matthew's gospel, while Luke presents a slightly softened challenge: "Be merciful, just as your Father is merciful." Which raises an important question: For a follower of Jesus, does the Sermon on the Mount set a standard so high that we are guaranteed to fail as we seek to meet it, thereby demonstrating our inherent imperfections? Or does Jesus rather present a standard that is a model for how a life of faith should be lived?

Although not a true "perfectionist," I have been driven by "perfectionism" in various areas of my life for as long as I can remember. Because I know from experience that perfectionism is a curse, I have always been made nervous by Jesus's "Be perfect" command in Matthew. I even have said in class, to the discomfort of my mostly Catholic students, "What the hell kind of a moral standard is that?" I am in good company, because philosopher and novelist Iris Murdoch once asked, "What of the command 'Be ye therefore perfect?' Would it not be more sensible to say 'Be ye therefore slightly improved?'" More than a decade earlier, she had built this tension into one of her novels.

The central structural pillars of Murdoch's novel *The Bell* are the dueling sermons of James and Michael on consecutive Sundays, rivals for the leadership of a lay religious community. James, on the one hand, is convinced that moral perfection is well within any human being's reach—we know what is required of us and just need to stop thinking about it and do it. Perfection is measured by the external standard given to us by God through Scripture and tradition. We fail to be perfect through weakness of will. Throughout the novel, James is also revealed as judgmental and self-righteous, rigidly insensitive to the nuances and realities of other people.

Michael, on the other hand, preaches that moral behavior begins with an honest assessment of one's limitations and imperfections—he says that "one must perform the lower act which one can manage and sustain: not the higher act which one bungles." Although Michael's position is far more humane and embraceable than James's, Michael's life is a series of continual missteps for which he seeks and expects immediate forgiveness from himself and others. When, due to his moral blundering, a member of the community commits suicide, Michael himself becomes suicidal as he realizes that his lazy acceptance of his own limitations has poisoned his relationships and caused him to blindly miss the importance of continually striving for perfection. Contentment with "slight improvement," in his case, has become identical with self-absorption and stagnation.

So there's the problem. How am I—how are we—to embrace imperfection while at the same time avoiding complacency? Jeanne, who is far wiser than I on these matters, believes that it has to do with "the law of love." Perfection is a deadly burden as long as it is a standard of judgment. But through the lens of love, it becomes something different. As long as my image of perfection involves avoiding judgment by making no mistakes, I live in fear and am doomed to failure. Alternatively, the growth inspired by taking risks and making mistakes without fear is directed toward a perfection of a very different sort.

Being a follower of Jesus requires, first and foremost, a willingness to stop judging ourselves and each other. It involves believing that we are called to live out our faith as both the recipients and bearers of divine love, a love we are called to bring into the world as we live our daily lives. We are not called to be perfect in the sense of never making mistakes. We are called to become unique incarnations of divine love, a love that cannot help but change everything that is within our reach. The wise

Abbess in *The Bell* tells Michael toward the end of the novel, "The idea of perfection moves, and possibly changes, us because it inspires love in the part of us that is most worthy." And as we read in 1 John, "perfect love casts out fear."

For reflection: Whether the Sermon on the Mount sets an impossible standard or one that is difficult but achievable has been a matter of debate for centuries. Which sort of standard is more likely to encourage growth and change?

Eighth Sunday After Epiphany: "Consider the lilies"

Year A: Matthew 6:24–34

The Epiphany 8 Year A gospel reading concludes several consecutive Sundays immersed in the Sermon on the Mount. The text includes passages almost as familiar as the Beatitudes:

No one can serve two masters . . . You cannot serve God and wealth.

Look at the birds of the air; they neither sow nor reap nor gather into barns, and yet your heavenly Father feeds them.

Consider the lilies of the field . . . they neither toil nor spin, yet even Solomon in all his glory was not clothed like one of these.

Do not worry about tomorrow, for tomorrow will bring worries of its own. Today's trouble is enough for today.

Anne Lamott tells the story of an older woman in the midst of a twelve-step recovery program. One of the steps involved a lengthy and elaborate prayer about turning your life and expectations over to God, whatever or whomever you understand God to be. The woman revealed that instead of this elaborate prayer, she and some of the other older folks simply prayed "Whatever" upon waking, and "Oh, well" before going to sleep. This woman had internalized Jesus's advice about worry and fear. Since we live in a world that is both frightening and largely out of our direct control, cultivating the habits of letting go and letting be is essential. As T. S. Eliot wrote in "Ash Wednesday,"

> *Teach us to care and not to care / Teach us to sit still.*

The challenge of learning both to care and not to care should be familiar to persons of faith—this dynamic is woven throughout sacred texts. Jesus says to stop worrying about tomorrow, not because it will all work out for the best, but rather because today will provide us with enough to worry about. The beauty of the lilies that are more splendidly clothed than Solomon in all his glory is fragile and temporary. We are assured that God is aware when even a lowly sparrow falls from its nest, yet we are not assured that God is doing anything to keep the sparrow from falling in the first place. "Whatever" and "Oh, well" can sometimes take on a sacred meaning.

Fear and worry turn us inward; when Jesus invites us to consider the natural world around us—lilies, sparrows, growing crops, the wind—he is asking us to turn our attention toward things other than ourselves. When Jesus consistently challenges us to pay attention to the "least of these," people falling through the cracks whose plight may seem distant from and unrelated to our own lives, he is calling us to full personhood. Iris Murdoch, who was an atheist, describes this dynamic in her essay "On 'God' and 'Good'":

> *Rilke said of Cezanne that he did not paint "I like it," he painted "There it is." One might say here that art is an excellent analogy of morals, or indeed that it is in this respect a case of morals. We cease to be in order to attend to the existence of something else, a natural object, a person in need.*

The ebb and flow of human existence is inexorable, suggesting that there might be better strategies for coping than immediately descending into worry and fear over the daily events, great and small, that threaten to snuff out even our most basic hopes and dreams. Learn how to engage with things as they are rather than as we wish them to be. Remember that we are not, after all, the center of the universe. Do not stifle the beauty and promise of a day by insisting that everything is ultimately about us. These are the lessons of the birds and the lilies.

On those days when hope seems most distant, when the promise of things getting better sounds empty, consider this passage from the middle of perhaps the darkest text in the Jewish Scriptures, the Book of Lamentations:

> *But this I call to mind, and therefore I have hope:*
> *The steadfast love of the Lord never ceases, his mercies never come to an end;*
> *They are new every morning; great is your faithfulness.*
> *"The Lord is my portion," says my soul, "therefore I will hope in him."*
> *The Lord is good to those who wait for him, to the soul that seeks him.*
> *It is good that one should wait quietly for the salvation of the Lord.*

Or, to put it differently, "whatever" and "oh well."

For reflection: *Once at a retreat the leader regularly said that the key to peace and centeredness is to "be where you are and do what you are doing." How does this advice compare to Jesus's advice to consider the lilies?*

Transfiguration Sunday: "Listen to Him"

Year A: Matthew 17:1–8; Year B: Mark 9:2–8; Year C: Luke 9:28–36

No matter how many Sundays the season of Epiphany contains in a given year, the last one is Transfiguration Sunday, coming just before Ash Wednesday and the beginning of Lent. Included in all three of the Synoptic Gospels, Jesus's transfiguration is a strange story with multiple layers of possible meaning. Jesus is worn out by the crowds and takes his inner circle, Peter, James, and John, with him to the top of a mountain for a break. While there, he is transfigured with Elijah and Moses. Matthew's gospel tells us that "His clothes became dazzling white," while Mark adds in his gospel that they were "whiter than anyone in the world could bleach them." Peter blurts out, "Let us put up three dwellings—one for you, one for Moses, and one for Elijah."

Why does Peter make such an apparently random suggestion? Luke tells us—"He did not know what he was saying." Far be it from Peter to say nothing when he doesn't know what to say, to look and attend to what's going on in silence and awe. No, he has to nail it down, organize it, put walls around it, and either sell tickets or write up a doctrinal statement and confession of faith. The voice from heaven makes it clear what Peter should be doing: *This is my Son, my Chosen; listen to him!*

"Look, don't touch." This used to be my mother's automatic command every time we walked into a store of any sort, from grocery to hardware to department. Every parent worth the job description has this command in her or his repertoire, knowing that precivilized human beings are inveterate grabbers. Hannah Arendt is reported to have said, "Every generation, civilization is invaded by barbarians—we call them 'children.'"

Absolutely true, and "Look, don't touch" is one of the earliest and best tools to use for domestication purposes. In truth, though, the temptation to look and grab, rather than simply to look, is one that none of us ever truly overcomes. As soon as we see something, we want to possess it, to make it ours and own it. That's what Peter is seeking to do with what he doesn't understand in the transfiguration story, when what he should be doing is looking, listening, and keeping his mouth shut.

Scripture makes it clear that there is a time to look and a time to touch—and don't confuse the two. In 2 Samuel, the newly crowned King David leads the army of Israel against the Philistines and recaptures the Ark of the Covenant. They place the Ark on an oxen-drawn cart and head back to Jerusalem in a parade complete with singing and musical instruments, led by David dancing "with all his might." The oxen step in a pothole and stumble, the Ark starts tipping off of the cart, and some poor guy named Uzzah makes the horrible mistake of assuming that he should put his hand on the Ark to steady it, because maybe God would just as soon not see the Ark lying on its side in the mud. God strikes Uzzah dead on the spot for his efforts. "Look, don't touch."

As a native New Englander, one of my all-time favorite stories is Nathaniel Hawthorne's "The Great Stone Face." It is the story of a boy named Ernest who lives in a New Hampshire valley; on the perpendicular side of a nearby mountain hang some immense rocks that, when viewed from the proper angle and distance, "precisely resembled the features of a human countenance." The valley is Franconia Notch in the middle of the White Mountains, only forty miles or so from where I grew up; "The Old Man of the Mountain," as we called it, was a regular point of destination for my family. I was crushed when a number of years ago, despite the best sustained preservation efforts, the old man finally fell off the mountain.

According to Hawthorne's story, there is a legend in the valley that someday

> *[a] child should be born hereabouts, who is destined to become the greatest and noblest personage of his time, and whose*

> *countenance, in manhood, should bear an exact resemblance to the Great Stone Face.*

Ernest, who gazes daily with love and awe at the Great Stone Face, spends his whole life as a simple laborer in the valley. Occasionally a rumor would arise that the man resembling the Great Stone Face had appeared in town, but each candidate—a wealthy miser, a vain general, a pompous politician—turned out to be a fraud. As the years pass and Ernest becomes an old man, he is loved by his neighbors and family, but he sadly concludes that the legend will not come true in his lifetime.

Then one day as he talks simply and clearly on his front porch with a number of his friends about matters important to all of them, the setting sun strikes Ernest's face and someone sitting next to him exclaims, "Behold! Behold! Ernest is himself the likeness of the Great Stone Face!" He had become what he had spent his life lovingly looking at.

Iris Murdoch tells us that "man is a creature who makes pictures of himself and then comes to resemble the picture." And the pictures we make will be fashioned from what we are looking at and what we see most clearly. Simone Weil writes, "To look and to eat are two different things. The only people who have any hope of salvation are those who occasionally stop and look for a time, instead of eating. Looking is what saves us." What are you looking at?

***For reflection:** In his letter to the Philippians, Paul suggests the sorts of things that we should be looking at and thinking about: "Finally, whatever things are true . . . honest . . . just . . . pure . . . lovely . . . of good report. If there is any virtue, if there is any praise, think on these things." Where in your life are you most likely to find things of this sort?*

CHAPTER

4

Lent—Beauty for Ashes

The season of Lent lasts for the forty days (not including the Sundays in Lent) between Ash Wednesday and Easter. It is a season of inwardness, self-reflection, penance, prayer, and preparation for the events of Holy Week and Easter. For a number of reasons, Lent was the most difficult liturgical season for me to embrace, partly because it has often been stereotypically characterized as a time during which one should give up important things in an attempt to, for a brief few weeks, be more "spiritual" than usual.

Over the years, I have discovered features of the season—features that very seldom are discussed in conversations about Lent—that are transferable to the daily human struggle regardless of what liturgical season one happens to be in. As Jeanne once pointed out to me, the question is not "What should I give up for Lent in order to feel deprived, and therefore more spiritual or holy?" The question rather is, "Do I dare treat myself as if I matter?" or "Am I willing to risk seeing myself as valued and loved in the way that God sees me?" If the answer to this is "yes," then what are the ways in which I habitually treat myself as if I did not matter? Am I willing to deliberately suspend those activities, even for a limited time?

Ash Wednesday: "To dust you shall return"

My initial encounter with Ash Wednesday was not promising. My first liturgical year was progressing beautifully, as I immersed myself in the hope and anticipation of Advent, enjoyed the Christmas season as I never had, and participated in the seminal texts of Jesus's coming out party during Epiphany.

Then Ash Wednesday happened. I remember it well. I regularly attended the 7:00 a.m. prayer service usually run by lay people, but this morning the dean was there. We went to a place in the prayer book I had never seen before and proceeded through the most depressing liturgy ever. I found myself in the aisle queuing up to receive ashes. As the dean traced a cross with his ash-covered finger on my forehead and said, "Vance, remember that you are dust, and to dust you shall return," I thought, "This time you've gone too far, Morgan. This is just too weird." I washed the ashes off my forehead as soon as I got home, convinced that I was never going to do *that* again.

The idea of Lent—a time in which persons of faith are challenged to give something up or take something on as a sign of renewed or deeper commitment to God—has always been a tough sell for me. I agree with Thomas Merton, who wrote that

> [t]he only trouble is that in the spiritual life there are no tricks and there are no shortcuts. Those who imagine that they can discover spiritual gimmicks and put them to work for themselves usually ignore God's will and his grace.

And Lent—a time set aside to "get serious" about faith in practice—can easily turn into such a gimmick.

I can give up anything for forty days, but whatever I choose to sacrifice, unless it is simply frivolous, is something that I should probably consider giving up for good. Whatever I choose to take on for forty days with the intent of becoming a temporarily better person is, if I am serious about my choice, something that I should undoubtedly seek to establish as a permanent part of my life.

The Ash Wednesday liturgy is somber and thought-provoking; for me, the most powerful portion of the liturgy is Psalm 51, read right after the imposition of ashes. Psalm 51 is a penitential psalm attributed to David, a plea for forgiveness and restoration written after the prophet Nathan called David out for committing adultery with Bathsheba, then arranging for Bathsheba's husband Uriah to be killed in battle:

Create in me a clean heart, O God,
and put a new and right spirit within me.
Do not cast me away from your presence,
and do not take your holy spirit from me.
Restore to me the joy of your salvation,
and sustain in me a willing spirit . . .
The sacrifice acceptable to God is a broken spirit;
a broken and contrite heart you will not despise.

David is described in the Jewish Scriptures as "a man after [God's] own heart," but he not only is imperfect but also frequently fails basic standards of moral goodness. His adultery with Bathsheba might be David's most famous transgression, but the stories in 1 and 2 Samuel make it clear that he is thoroughly flawed—violent, occasionally murderous, vain, manipulative, and in love with power. Psalm 51 is a plea from the depths of the heart of one who, despite his failures, continually seeks relationship with God.

Ash Wednesday and Lent remind us that our human failings and our human hunger for what is greater than us go equally deep. This can be addressed neither by a mere few weeks of sacrifice nor by the expectation that surface-level actions and words will suffice. Despite David's fervent prayers and fasting, the son born of his adultery with Bathsheba died. And yet the second child of their union was Solomon, the next king of Israel.

I have learned over many years of struggling with Lent that the life of faith, the life of seeking God, is incremental and daily. The liturgical calendar provides a different color and atmosphere for this daily process: hope and expectation for Advent, self-reflection for Lent, joy for Easter, and so on. But hope, reflection, and joy (and a whole bunch of other things) need to be part of my daily travels with the divine. Dropping bad habits and attitudes cannot wait until Lent, and neither can the addition of new habits and attitudes that my commitment to the life of faith calls for.

For reflection: What role has Ash Wednesday played in your life of faith? What does "a broken and contrite heart" from Psalm 51 mean to you?

First Sunday in Lent: Temptation

Year A: Matthew 4:1–11; Year B: Mark 1:12–13; Year C: Luke 4:1–13

The Gospel reading for Lent 1 in all three liturgical years is the account of Jesus's forty days of temptation in the wilderness from one of the Synoptic Gospels. Mark's version is only two verses long, while Matthew and Luke provide a fuller treatment, including the three challenges posed to Jesus by the devil.

This story is the centerpiece of one of the greatest passages in all of Western literature, Fyodor Dostoevsky's tale of the Grand Inquisitor in *The Brothers Karamazov*. What if, Dostoevsky wonders, Jesus had succumbed to one of the temptations? Might things have been better in the long run? The story is a profound meditation on what Jesus's true message was and what human beings have done with it over the succeeding millennia.

Dostoevsky asks us to imagine that Jesus unexpectedly shows up in sixteenth-century Seville during the height of the Spanish Inquisition. Although "[h]e appeared quietly, inconspicuously," everyone recognizes him and immediately starts bringing those who are sick and disabled to him to be healed. The Grand Inquisitor, an old and severe man "almost ninety . . . with a gaunt face and sunken eyes from which a glitter shines like a fiery spark," watches from the sidelines. When Jesus raises a young girl from the dead as her funeral procession passes by, the Inquisitor has had enough. He motions to his guards, the crowd parts, and Jesus is taken into custody.

What follows is an extraordinary monologue in which for several pages the Inquisitor rails against a silent Jesus for having returned to mess up everything that future generations of his claimed followers have accomplished in the fifteen hundred years since Jesus left. From the perspective of the Roman Catholic Church, which the Inquisitor represents, Jesus's original message that human beings have the freedom to choose to follow and be in relationship with God was both elitist and misguided.

The Inquisitor argues that the vast majority of human beings do not *want* to be free. Rather, they will predictably turn their freedom over to the nearest authority who promises security and safety in exchange for that freedom. Jesus's message, in other words, is based on a profound misreading of human nature. We are by nature too weak to handle freedom and the responsibility that goes with it. All we really want is for someone to tell us what to do, remove the responsibility of choice from us, and take care of us.

The Inquisitor uses the three temptations as described in Luke's gospel to frame his monologue. In his estimation, the three challenges thrown by the devil at Jesus "express in three words, in three human phrases only, the entire future history of the world and mankind." Consider, for instance, what really is contained in the first temptation—"If you are the Son of God, turn these stones into bread"—which the Inquisitor expansively rephrases as follows:

> *You want to go into the world, and you are going empty-handed, with some promise of freedom, which they in their simplicity and innate lawlessness cannot even comprehend, which they dread and fear . . . But do you see these stones? Turn them into bread and mankind will run after you like sheep, grateful and obedient.*

The Inquisitor knows that obedience bought with bread is not obedience freely given, but so what? Human beings are not only incapable of handling freedom, but they also don't want it in the first place. He argues that our greatest concern is to find someone or something to whom we can give our freedom in exchange for escaping the responsibility that accompanies freedom.

What do human beings desire more, freedom or security? Choice or to be taken care of? These questions have challenged philosophers and theologians for millennia. Jesus's answer to the devil's first temptation in Luke's gospel, of course, is "man does not live by bread alone." There are more important things, in other words, than having your physical needs taken care of and feeling secure. Freedom, for instance. The Inquisitor is shocked that the Son of God could have misread human nature so badly.

> *You objected that man does not live by bread alone, but do you know that in the name of this very earthly bread, the spirit of the earth will rise against you and fight with you and defeat you, and everyone will follow him exclaiming, "Who can compare to this beast, for he has given us fire from heaven!" . . . Feed them first, then ask virtue of them.*

In the Inquisitor's estimation, the work of religious authorities for the fifteen centuries since Jesus's first appearance (and arguably for the next six since the Inquisitor) has been to reshape and adjust Jesus's message into something more in tune with what human beings actually *are* rather than some hopeful and stylized vision of what they might be. He tells Jesus that

> *[h]ad you accepted the "loaves," you would have answered the universal and everlasting anguish of man as an individual being . . . namely "before whom shall I bow down?" There is no more ceaseless or tormenting care for man, as long as he remains free, than to find someone to bow down to as soon as possible.*

This presents a powerful challenge that raises important questions for every person who claims to be a follower of Jesus. Do I truly understand how radical and challenging the call of the gospel is? Am I really capable of accepting the responsibility that goes along with freely seeking to live out a life of faith in real time? Wouldn't it be much better simply to turn that freedom and accompanying responsibility over to someone or something else—a church, a political party, an authority figure, or a social construct that will break the life of faith down into manageable proportions in exchange for my obedience and submission to their demands? Ultimately, what am I looking for? Freedom or security? Radical open-endedness or certainty? Risk or safety?

From his prison cell just weeks before his execution by the Nazis, Dietrich Bonhoeffer wrote, "When Christ calls a man, he bids him come and die." That's the sort of thing that the Grand Inquisitor says is far too demanding and difficult for human beings. Was he right?

For reflection: Think of times when you have felt insecure and uncertain. Do you rely on your faith to provide certainty in such times, or do you believe that faith and uncertainty are natural companions on life's journey?

Second Sunday in Lent: "God so loved the world"

Year A: John 3:1–17

The Year A gospel reading for Lent 2 is from John 3; it contains what many have described as "the gospel in a nutshell." John 3:16 is perhaps the most familiar of all Bible verses, the first scripture verse (followed by hundreds more) that I memorized as a young Baptist boy. This is the King James Version (KJV) as I learned it:

> *For God so loved the world, that He gave His only begotten Son, that whosoever believeth in Him should not perish but have everlasting life.*

In our fundamentalist, evangelical world, the whole gospel was summed up in this verse, often followed by its less quoted companion John 3:17 (also in the KJV):

> *For God sent not His Son into the world to condemn the world, but that the world through Him might be saved.*

These verses really do have it all—a God of salvation rather than condemnation, of love rather than judgment, the Incarnation, and—most important in the religious world of my youth—the promise of eternal life, which we interpreted as going to heaven and avoiding hell.

John's gospel is strange and (for me, least) takes a bit of getting used to. It was written last of the four Gospels, at least twenty years later than Matthew and Luke, perhaps thirty years later than Mark. The Jesus of John often sounds more like a theology professor who likes to talk a lot than the no-nonsense man of few words and mighty deeds in Mark's gospel.

In John chapter 3, Jesus is visited secretly at night by Nicodemus, "a ruler of the Jews" who was a Pharisee and a member of the Sanhedrin—in other words, a significant player in the religious and political structure that Jesus was clearly challenging. Nicodemus comes by night undoubtedly because he does not want his colleagues to know of his fascination with Jesus. He provides an opening that Jesus takes advantage of by saying cryptically, "Except a man be born again, he cannot see the kingdom of God." We Baptists took this to mean that "unless you accept Jesus into your heart as your personal Lord and Savior, you don't get to go to heaven" (although Jesus doesn't say this), but the "eternal life" business isn't what catches Nicodemus's attention.

Taking the "born again" line literally, he wants to know: "How can a man be born when he is old? Can he enter the second time into his mother's womb and be born?" Debates were raging in Jesus's world between the Pharisees and the Sadducees about whether resurrection of the dead is possible. Nicodemus, familiar with those debates, thinks Jesus is taking a position. But he isn't. He's talking about something else entirely.

As the conversation continues, Jesus reminds Nicodemus of the strange story from the history of the children of Israel wandering in the desert from the Book of Numbers. Reacting to yet another round of blatant disobedience, God sends poisonous snakes into the midst of the children of Israel; many of those bitten by the venomous serpents die. In response to the people's recognition of their rebellion and their penitence, God instructs Moses to craft a serpent of bronze and lift it on a pole for everyone to see. "And so it was, if a serpent had bitten anyone, when he looked at the bronze serpent, he lived."

Applying the story to himself thousands of years later, Jesus tells Nicodemus that "as Moses lifted up the serpent in the wilderness, even so must the Son of Man be lifted up." Which sheds a whole new light on John 3:16 just two verses later. Jesus is not talking about crawling back into your mother's womb, nor is he talking about going to heaven when you die. He is talking about the importance of what we choose to look at. Jesus is telling Nicodemus, and is telling us, that the possibility of transformation and renewal is right in front of us—but our attention is usually focused elsewhere.

It's interesting to note that John 3:16 does not require us to do anything but believe. No deeds need to be performed, no special words need to be said, no special prayers need to be offered, no sins need to be confessed. Just believe. I spent many years trying to figure out what I needed *to do* to earn God's favor. As it turns out, belief is about focusing my attention on the right thing. Not on my shortcomings and failings, nor on my strengths and what I think I have to offer that God might be able to use. Jesus's message to Nicodemus is very similar to the voice from heaven's message to Peter at the transfiguration. "Don't act—LOOK."

Nicodemus's conversation with Jesus clearly had an impact; we see him two more times in John's narrative, once when he reminds his brethren in the Sanhedrin that the law requires that a person be heard before being judged, the second time when he assists Joseph of Arimathea in preparing Jesus's body for burial after the crucifixion. He did not drop everything he was doing and start following Jesus, but he did begin to see things differently.

We would do well to wonder the same things that Nicodemus must have wondered about. Where do I usually focus my attention? What would it mean to shift my gaze toward something different? What would it mean to stop looking at the shortcomings, failures, and sins in my own life and the lives of those around me? What would it be like to stop staring a few inches in front of me as I sleepwalk through my days and weeks and look up? What difference would it make if I looked at the promise of life rather than the inevitability of death? The bronze serpent lifted in the wilderness. The Son of Man hanging on a cross. Both are iconic images of God's love and forgiveness, promising that new life can be ours *now*, that the kingdom of God is available *now*, and eternal life begins *now*. All we need to do is look.

For reflection: In Acts 16, after Paul and Silas are miraculously released from prison, the jailer asks them "Sirs, what must I do to be saved?" They reply, "Believe on the Lord Jesus Christ and you will be saved, and your household." How does Paul and Silas's answer compare to what Jesus says in John 3?

Third Sunday in Lent: Wells of water

Year A: John 4:5–42

The gospel reading for Lent 3 Year A is John's account of Jesus's encounter with the Samaritan woman at the well. In the last episode of season one of *The Chosen,* Jesus deliberately travels with his growing entourage through Samaria, even though it lengthens their journey considerably. Samaritans hate Jews as much as Jews hate Samaritans. When his disciples question his choice, Jesus simply says, "There's someone there whom I want to meet." His conversation with the woman at the well is not only one of the first times that Jesus reveals his identity as the Messiah to a non-Jewish person, but also has been the source for foundational Christian theology over the centuries.

One does not get very far reading in the Bible without encountering a well. In a largely desert landscape, wells were both the source of life and the center of community activity. Isaac and Rebekah met at a well, as did Jacob and Rachel, as well as Moses and Zipporah. Joseph's older brothers threw him into a dried-up well after he offended them one too many times. Battles were fought over wells. They are so prevalent and necessary in stories from a nomadic, arid land that it's easy to imagine that they are natural parts of the landscape. But they aren't. A well is a human attempt to harness something very necessary but also very powerful—a spring of water.

In ancient texts, springs and sources of water are sacred. This is not surprising, because water is necessary for life. A spring—an oasis—stands for life, for rest and refreshment. But it is the random power of a spring that most directly brings the divine to mind. Springs are as resistant to our attempts to control them as they are to our expectations. Just when we think that we have water under control, it decides to go somewhere else. It turns every apparent barrier into a new channel.

This would be good to remember every time I think I have God figured out, whenever my path to a frequently visited well becomes a bit too often travelled. The divine spring has a mind and will of its own, and if I don't pay attention, I will find my well, so carefully built to contain the spring, empty one day. And this is not a good thing—as Peter wrote, "[T]hese are waterless springs... for them the deepest darkness has been reserved."

The prophet Isaiah captures the impossibility of either controlling or predicting God's thoughts or intentions:

> *For my thoughts are not your thoughts, nor are your ways my ways, says the LORD. For as the heavens are higher than the earth, so are my ways higher than your ways and my thoughts than your thoughts.*

It is easy to forget that the divine spring was never intended to be contained permanently in any external well, whether a building, a book, or a specific location. The good news, as Jesus told the woman at the well, is that the divine spring is "a well of water springing up into everlasting life." And that well is me. And you. It's a great idea—portable wells containing the most life-giving water ever imagined. I need go no further than where I happen to be to find out what the divine spring is doing.

For reflection: One of Jesus's consistent messages throughout his ministry was that God is not to be found in specific locations or buildings; rather, God is to be found in human beings who seek to be followers of God in real time. What are the

implications of this for our attempts to build and sustain worship communities?

Fourth Sunday in Lent: The prodigal son

Year C: Luke 15:1–3, 11–32

At the beginning of the Lent 4 Year C gospel reading from Luke, the Pharisees and scribes complain that many of the people attracted to Jesus's teachings are tax collectors and similarly disreputable persons. "This fellow welcomes sinners and eats with them," the Pharisees and scribes grumble. Jesus responds with a series of familiar parables, including the lost sheep, the lost coin, the dishonest manager, and the rich man and Lazarus. In the middle of these stories is perhaps Jesus's best-known parable (along with the Good Samaritan), the story of the prodigal son. When a story is this familiar, it is often important to shake things up a bit in order to gain new insights.

Suppose the person in the pulpit on Lent 4 summarized the story in this way:

> *This young guy asks his wealthy father for his inheritance early, gets it, leaves home and union with his father, then squanders his inheritance in riotous living—sex, drugs, alcohol, you name it. He ends up working with the pigs, which for a Jewish audience means that he can't sink any lower. He thinks it's all over. He thinks he's going to die.*
>
> *But then this guy Jesus comes along, finds the guy among the pigs, and says, "Look, I'll walk you back to your father. Now, I know your father. He's judgmental, he's powerful, he holds a grudge, and he's going to need someone to be tortured and murdered for this nonsense that you did. We all know that your father is an unreasonable tyrant. Someone's going to have to pay for what you did; heads are going to roll.*

> But I'll go in with you, I'll plead your case to your father. I'll say, "I know you want to kill your son for what he did, but kill me instead." And he does. He tortures and murders Jesus and then the prodigal son is safe to come home.

Any person familiar with the story, of course, will say, "That's not how the story goes!" But the father in this retelling of the story is behaving precisely as the God that many of us were taught to believe in behaves. God is judgmental, God cannot abide disobedience and sin, so Jesus has to die as an atoning sacrifice for those sins and to appease God who, perhaps grudgingly, accepts us back into divine good favor only after the sacrifice of Jesus. If the father in the prodigal son parable stands for God, as virtually all interpreters of the story say he *should*, then given what we've been taught to believe concerning God this is how the story goes.

But it doesn't. Instead, while knee deep in the muck of the pigsty, the son remembers his father. I'm his son. Maybe if I go back he'll at least let me be a servant and have a place to stay. He does go back, his father sees him "from afar off," runs to him, and embraces him. The prodigal son has a little speech prepared, but the father says, "Whatever. You were dead and now you're alive again! Let's have a party!"

Of course, that isn't the whole story. The older son, who has been the "good" son his whole life and done everything his father asked of him, is entirely put out when he returns from the fields and hears the party going on. The older son's response to his father's unlimited forgiveness toward the reprobate son is perfectly understandable, but is also self-important and judgmental. The older brother in the story clearly represents the Pharisees and others who consider themselves to be in good standing with God. In similar situations elsewhere in the Gospels, Jesus calls them out for their hypocrisy, hubris, and self-righteousness, but in this story the father does not judge the older brother. Instead, he invites his eldest son to enter with him into joy and celebration over the prodigal son, who "was lost and has been found." Above all else, the prodigal son story establishes God's nature as wildly loving, forgiving, and inclusive.

My father once gave me a book to read when I was in my middle school/high school years. It was a small theological classic; J. B. Phillips's *Your God Is Too Small*. Each brief chapter describes a God of limited imagination: a policeman God, a projection of your parents, a God of perpetual grievance, and more. I recall little of the content more than five decades later, but the concept in the title has stayed with me ever since. If your God is all justice and no mercy, all righteousness and no love, you might want to stretch your imagination a bit. If your friend can forgive you for your worst behavior but your God cannot without blood sacrifice, you need a different God. As J. B. Phillips would have said, your God is too small.

For reflection: Why do you think Jesus so often responded to direct questions or criticisms with parables and stories? What does this say about the nature of God? About human nature?

Fifth Sunday in Lent: The raising of Lazarus

Year A: Ezekiel 37:1–14, John 11:1–45

The gospel for Lent 5 Year A, the last Sunday before Palm Sunday, transitions us into Holy Week, and focuses on what could be described as Jesus's signature miracle—the raising of Lazarus. The story always makes me nostalgic for various Hollywood treatments of Jesus's life from my youth. One of the most memorable is the 1966 film *The Greatest Story Ever Told*, directed by George Stevens.

Stevens hinges the whole three-hour-plus spectacle on the raising of Lazarus, which takes place just over halfway through the movie. Instead of focusing on Jesus and Lazarus, the camera focuses on the reactions of those present. Shocked faces, stunned silence, a woman drops to her knees, a man bursts into tears. One witness runs down the road toward Jerusalem, grabbing random people and sharing the news—"Jesus of Nazareth . . . I saw it, I saw it with my own eyes! Lazarus was dead, and now he's alive!" "The Messiah has come! A man was dead, and now he lives!"

If this is Jesus's career-defining miracle, why is it only reported in one of the four canonical Gospels? Why do Matthew, Mark, and Luke not consider the story important enough to include in their narratives? Why does Jesus deliberately delay travelling to Bethany upon hearing that his friend is deathly ill? We know a lot about Jesus with Lazarus's sisters, Mary and Martha, but this is the first time we've heard about Lazarus. Is he the domineering older brother of Mary and Martha, or the spoiled younger brother on whom they dote? Why does Jesus weep? What happened to Lazarus after he was raised from the dead? How did he live out the rest of his life?

The story of Lazarus is our story, the story of everyone who seeks, in individual and unique ways, to be friends with Jesus. The Lent 5 Year A selection from the Jewish Scriptures is the prophet Ezekiel's vision of a valley of dry bones. We all, I suspect, have spiritually experienced a valley-of-dry-bones season. Dry bones are the remaining evidence of something that was once alive but hasn't been for a long time. Each of us has been through a "dark night," a time in which everything relied upon turns out to be unreliable, and everything that made sense no longer does. Let's look at an example.

I claim to be a follower of Jesus, but the internal flame has slowly decreased to an ember that is threatening to die out. I haven't seen or talked with Jesus, or really spent time with him, for a while. Those closest to me might realize that something's wrong but are unable to help. Nothing but silence. And deep down, I know this is not just a dry period, a time in the desert.

The spiritual ember flickers out, leaving a cold, empty space full of ashes at my core. This is real death, from which there is no return. "Lazarus is dead."

As noted in a previous section, Dietrich Bonhoeffer once wrote that "[w]hen Christ calls a man, he bids him come and die." And death is not attractive. It isn't pretty. No matter how beautiful the dress, how snazzy the suit, how professional the make-up job, a corpse is still a corpse. Spiritual corpses go through the motions, pretending that "there's still some life left in these bones," but deep down they know it's a lie. "My bones are dried up, and my hope is gone. I am cut off completely."

But after what seems like a spiritual eternity—a rattling of bones, a puff of breath—there are the stirrings of life. I've been dead for so long, I'm disoriented. I don't recognize my surroundings, nor the voice in the distance. "Come forth!" As a moth toward a flame, I'm drawn toward that sound, toward a pinpoint of light, and I find that, against all odds, what was dead is alive again. I'm surrounded by those I thought I had lost, those whom I'd thought I would never truly see again. "We thought you were dead!" "I was!" But I can't move properly, can't see clearly, I feel like a mummy who just became alive again. And I hear a commanding voice: "Loose him, and let him go."

I've been raised to new life—so why am I still bound by the vestiges of death, by the graveclothes of a past that I thought was gone? Because spiritual renewal and growth are like the evolutionary process—I drag the remnants of a past reality into my new life. Vestiges of what has died still remain. If inattentive, I will attempt to weave new garments of salvation out of old, stinking rags that have long outlived their purpose. And I cannot remove them by myself—I need help. I need the help of those who love me and who know what it's like to try to get one's bearings as a newly resurrected corpse. And the Lazarus cycle goes on.

The message of the story of Lazarus is "Don't be afraid to die"—especially to those things we cannot bear to even think about losing. Don't be afraid to release even what seems most necessary—familiar thoughts, comfortable patterns of behavior, toxic relationships, habits set in stone, well-intentioned but self-centered expectations—the very things that for each of us seem to be the cornerstone of existence. To truly live, we have to die. As Simone Weil wrote,

> *They alone will see God who prefer to recognize the truth and die, instead of living a long and happy existence in a state of illusion. One must want to go towards reality; then, when one thinks one has found a corpse5, one meets an angel who says: "He is risen."*

For reflection: C. S. Lewis once wrote that the person of Christian faith should be prepared to "die before you die." Consider what he might have meant in the context of the raising of Lazarus story.

CHAPTER 5

Holy Week—From Hosanna to Sepulcher

Things don't get much more dramatic than the events of Holy Week from Palm Sunday through Holy Saturday. Each Christian tradition has its own ways of addressing the powerful and poignant stories told in the Gospels. In some traditions, Holy Week is considered to be the last week of Lent rather than a separate liturgical season, while others consider Holy Week to be its own season. Either way, the events of Holy Week are so central to Christian belief that it deserves its own chapter.

As I have experienced Holy Week liturgies over the years, I have found that they almost always speak directly to what is going on in my life at the time. For while the Christian narrative is a cosmic and universal one, its meaning and impact often is radically individual.

Palm Sunday: From palms to Passion

Liturgy of the Palms: A: Matthew 21:1–11; B: Mark 11:1–11; C: Luke 19:20–48
Liturgy of the Passion: A: Matthew 26:14–27:66; B: Mark 14:1–15:47; C: Luke 22:14–23:56

Most everyone knows that Palm Sunday celebrates Jesus's riding triumphantly into Jerusalem on a donkey (or colt) as adoring crowds wave palm branches and shout "Hosanna," but the "Liturgy of the Palms" occupies only the first fifteen minutes or so of one of the most dramatic liturgies in the liturgical cycle. The priest reads the appointed gospel, the ushers distribute palms while everyone sings "All Glory, Laud and Honor" or something similar, the reading from the Jewish Scriptures, Psalm, and New Testament readings for the day are delivered.

Then the liturgical transmission shifts from fifth to second gear without a clutch. The "Liturgy of the Passion" begins as various assigned parishioners read the Passion story from the gospel and the joy of Jesus's triumphant entry transitions into the drama and tragedy of the coming week, a week that ends with Joseph of Arimathea providing a tomb for Jesus's body. Over the years I have read the roles of the narrator, Pontius Pilate, Herod, and the second thief, joining the congregation in the role of the "crowd," saying things like "We have no king but Caesar!" and "Crucify Him!" when not reading a specific role. But one Palm Sunday was particularly memorable.

After a challenging week at work, I was strongly tempted to skip church on Sunday morning for the first time in months. But it was Palm Sunday, and Jeanne was scheduled to be chalice bearer at the altar, so my Protestant guilt kicked in and off to church I went. As I entered the back of the church, the rector, a very good friend, was looking dramatic in her red chasuble as she waited to process to the front with the servers, readers, and choir.

Motioning me over, she whispered, "Do you want to read?" *Not really*, I thought as I looked to see what roles for the upcoming Passion reading were still available. Just about all of them, as it turned out, including the role of Jesus. "I'll be Jesus," I sighed. "I've never gotten to read his part."

"I'll be Jesus." That's really what it boils down to for those of us who have signed on to the project of trying to live out a serious Christian faith commitment. Holy Week is a time that many try to virtually "walk in the steps of Jesus" liturgically in the various special services. But to actually be God in the world, to be the vehicle through which the divine makes contact with our human reality—that's a different matter altogether. No wonder we are so creative in finding ways to make the demands of the life of faith more manageable.

My own attempts to avoid the challenges of what I claim to take seriously are regularly exposed by the prison letters of twentieth-century Lutheran pastor and theologian Dietrich Bonhoeffer. In the months between his imprisonment and his execution by the Nazis, Bonhoeffer wrote dozens of letters to his best friend, Eberhard Bethge, letters in which he explored and pressed the boundaries of his Christian faith in ways that have challenged and shocked readers ever since. Bonhoeffer asks, "What do we really believe? I mean, believe in such a way that we stake our lives on it?" These letters cause me to think about and look at the Holy Week narrative very differently.

Underlying the liturgies and activities between Palm Sunday and Easter is a shocking story in which "God lets the divine self be pushed out of the world onto the cross." God is apparently either unwilling or unable to engage with the suffering and pain of the world other than to become part of it. If the dramatic events of Jesus's final days are models for our lives in a suffering and distressed world, it is clear that, as Bonhoeffer writes, "Christ helps us, not by virtue of his omnipotence, but by virtue of his weakness and suffering."

I remember a rather dramatic solo that my aunt used to sing in the church of my youth almost every year at some point leading up to Easter that includes the line "he could have called ten thousand angels, but he died alone for you and me." If we take all of the accretions of dogma and doctrine out of the picture, the story of Jesus's last days is a disaster—as I read that Palm Sunday morning during the Passion narrative in Matthew's gospel, the final words Jesus gasps from the cross are, "My God, my God, why have you forsaken me?" Precisely the question Bonhoeffer must have been asking from his prison cell.

For reflection: Which portions of Holy Week liturgical observances have been most meaningful in your faith walk?

Monday of Holy Week: "You always have the poor"

Years A, B, C: John 12:1–11

The primary gospel readings for the weekdays in Holy Week are from John's gospel, with an alternative reading for each day from one of the Synoptic Gospels. John does not include a number of familiar stories from Holy Week that appear in the other three Gospels (Jesus driving the money changers from the temple and Jesus killing the fig tree, for instance); as with the birth-of-Jesus narratives, one needs to pay attention to all four Gospels to get the full story.

For those who claim to be guided by Christian principles, the gospel message is clear. In his reported teachings, Jesus never wavers from the message that in the divine economy and social structure, the poor, the widows, and the orphans—the disenfranchised and those who continually fall through the cracks, in other words—are to be considered first. If there is one thing that guarantees divine judgment, it is the failure to show paramount concern for "the least of these." The poorest deserve the best.

All of which makes the gospel reading for Monday of Holy Week challenging. Jesus is in Bethany at the house of Mary, Martha, and the newly raised Lazarus having dinner. The accounts in Matthew's and Mark's gospels say that this dinner was at the house of Simon the Leper and do not name the woman who anoints Jesus, but we can leave that for New Testament scholars to sort out. During the dinner, Mary brings an alabaster jar containing spikenard, a rare and expensive ointment, to Jesus, breaks the jar, and anoints Jesus's feet with the ointment (Matthew and Mark say Jesus's head is anointed). Mary's actions earn well-aimed criticism from the disciples and others present. "Why this waste of perfume? It could have been sold for more than a year's wages and the money given to the poor." And these critics were absolutely right. As those present understood Jesus's teaching, what Mary did was a violation of what has come be known as the "preferential option for the poor."

Which makes Jesus's response to the criticisms all the more surprising:

Leave her alone. She bought it so that she might keep it for the day of my burial. You always have the poor with you, but you do not always have me.

Not exactly what the group at dinner expected, I imagine. How to explain this apparent moment of self-centeredness? I have heard many theological explanations for Jesus's dismissive comment about the poor; I have even heard this very scene twisted into a justification for not funding social programs intended to help those in need.

Why do "the poorest deserve the best"? Not because they are in some strange way better than those who are not poor, but because, bottom line, *all* of us are incurably impoverished. Humanity itself suffers from poverty, the moral and imaginative poverty that time and again reproduces the same patterns of fear and violence. Despite our delusions of independence and self-made success, not one of us, not even the most financially secure and successful or confident law-abiding and godly person, can in truth look after ourselves.

The genius of the Christian narrative is that this is not only okay, but actually is the *reason* that God became human. In the Jewish Scriptures, God frequently tells the children of Israel that they have been chosen precisely *because* they are slaves and exiles, the most helpless community on the face of the earth. And this is why the poor are to be preferred—they are a constant reminder of the basic condition we all share.

This is also why we will always have the poor with us, why they will always stubbornly resist our best efforts to solve their problems. The poor will always be with us because we cannot escape our collective human impoverishment with exclusively human tools and strategies. Our giant goes with us wherever we go. The divine response? God does not let us have what is left over from the grace given to holy and honorable people. God doesn't look around for some small bonus that might come from the end-of-year surplus in the budget. God instead becomes one of us, an energizing force for change and reform that we cannot even imagine.

For reflection: We often think of "poverty" in exclusively economic terms, but consider the ways in which each person, even the most financially secure, is impoverished in ways that cannot simply be "fixed." Compare this to the first of the Beatitudes: "Blessed are the poor in spirit, for theirs is the kingdom of heaven."

Tuesday of Holy Week: Righteous anger

Year A, B, C: Mark 11:15–19

In all three of the Synoptic Gospels, the first thing that Jesus does early in Holy Week is drive the buyers, sellers, and moneychangers out of the Temple, overturning their tables and causing a general ruckus. Both Matthew and Mark also report that on one of the early days of Holy Week, Jesus cursed a fig tree because it had all leaves and no figs, even though it was not the right season for figs; the tree subsequently withered and died. Thousands of pages of commentary have been written seeking to provide the "real meaning" of these and similarly familiar events, but one thing is immediately clear from these stories: Jesus occasionally got angry.

For those who believe that Jesus was fully human, this should not be a surprise, given that anger is a typical and frequent human emotion. We also know that anger is one of the most dangerous human emotions, often leading to destructive and ill-advised actions. In the religious world of my youth, we were very uncomfortable with the possibility of Jesus's being angry. We reserved the term "righteous anger" for situations in which we could not explain Jesus's anger away easily.

Let's assume there is such a thing as "righteous anger." Jesus's cleansing of the Temple is often pointed to by Christians as the primary proof that sometimes anger is justified and appropriate. But no one ever has suggested that his one-off anger episode changed anything permanently; chances are the moneylenders and sacrificial animal vendors were back on the job the next day. Justified anger is directed, as the phrase indicates, at injustice— something our society and our world is full of. Justice is one of the highest of human virtues, and we seem hardwired to recognize when it is violated, even though there is seldom agreement about what justice would even look like.

Anger has been a staple of the political landscape for so long that many have concluded that it is the only possible emotion energetic enough to fuel real change. It is difficult to effect change when the people you need in the trenches of the revolution are relatively satisfied with the way things are going. What if the French peasants and working classes had said, "Well, things really aren't that bad" in 1780s France? What if the majority of American colonists had thought, "Actually, I can sort of see why the British Parliament wants to tax us without representation"? Of such attitudes a revolution is not made. Must anger and dissatisfaction be the primary driving forces behind meaningful change?

The prophet Micah writes that what God requires of us is to do justice, love kindness (mercy), and walk humbly with our God. But in many ways, Jesus's message in the Gospels transcends both justice and mercy, opening the door to something altogether different: grace. Justice is about fairness and mercy is about choosing to treat those who have done injustice as if they had not done so. But grace is something altogether different, an awareness that, in human hands, justice is often a zero-sum game, a game whose rules have to be rewritten if we are ever to establish true change.

Grace empowers a vision of human reality in which individuals are not lumped into categories, in which justice is not calculated mathematically, in which fairness is energized by a recognition of equal dignity rather than rights and entitlements, and which, as novelist and essayist Marilynne Robinson writes, inspires "the intimation of a great reality of another order, which pervades human experience, even manifests itself in human actions and relations, yet is always purely itself."

Those inspired by grace rather than justice must realize that grace cannot be institutionalized. Although a world or society of perfect justice has never existed, most human beings can imagine what such a society might look like—some of the great works of literature and philosophy provide us with glimpses. Grace is of a completely different order, calling for individuals and collectives to bring a transcendent, divinely inspired energy into mundane human activity.

When Jesus advocates perspectives and actions that make little common sense but are strangely attractive and beautiful, he's describing grace. We engage with it and come to understand it more effectively and deeply through parables, stories, and examples rather than rules and moral principles. And it cannot be systematized. But the good news is that it is applicable everywhere.

For reflection: As noted in a previous section, Anne Lamott writes that grace is when "suddenly you're in a different universe from the one where you were stuck, and there was absolutely no way for you to get there on your own." What are some examples of grace in your own life?

Wednesday of Holy Week: Betrayal or denial?

Years A, B, C: John 13:21–32

The appointed gospel for Wednesday of Holy Week takes us to a dramatic scene in the middle of Jesus's last meal with his disciples before his arrest (the early portions of the last supper narrative are the beginning of the gospel text for Maundy Thursday). The reading begins with Jesus observing that "one of you will betray me" and, a few verses later, ends with Jesus telling Simon Peter that "before the cock crows, you will have denied me three times." Judas betrayed Jesus, while Peter denied him. In traditional interpretations, we reject Judas, considering him the villain of the story, while resonating with Peter's weakness and ultimate repentance. But which is the greater temptation: betrayal or denial?

Kate Bowler's recent book *Good Enough*, co-written with Jessica Ritchie, got me thinking about aspects of this narrative that I thought had nothing new to offer. Bowler is an associate professor of the history of Christianity at Duke Divinity School, a position that she describes as her "dream job," which she says "has always felt like the purest expression of who I am." I not only understand Kate Bowler's love of the academic life and the privilege of participating in it—I could have written the preceding description myself.

With that in mind, it is somewhat of a shock when Bowler continues by saying that "I have the kind of life that is perfectly suited to idolatry of the highest order." Her subsequent discussion of idolatry connects in interesting ways to the stories of both Judas's betrayal and Peter's denial. She defines idolatry not as the following of false gods, but rather as becoming comfortable with false images of the true God. Her subsequent discussion of the distinction between idolatry and true faith reminds me of Dietrich Bonhoeffer's distinction between "cheap" and "costly" grace, where cheap grace is largely an intellectual commitment to a watered-down version of faith, while costly grace is "the treasure in the field" for which a person will give everything, even their life.

Why might a comfortable, successful life in a vocation that one considers identity-defining be "perfectly suited" to idolatry? To illustrate, Bowler looks to the most famous story of idolatry in the Jewish Scriptures, the golden calf narrative from the book of Exodus. Moses has been up on the mountain for an unexpectedly long time and the people of Israel are getting antsy. Moses's older brother, Aaron—the designated high priest and religious leader—agrees to oversee the fashioning of the golden calf idol, and we all know how well that worked out.

Bowler notes that neither Aaron nor the children of Israel consider the calf to be a false god—they are not breaking the first commandment to "have no other gods before me." Rather, they believe that this is an acceptable placeholder for the true god. That they are wrong about that makes them idolaters, even though they have not turned their backs on God in search of other gods. As Bowler describes it, "They did not create an image of a false God. They created a *false* image of the *true* God."

For those of us who live relatively comfortable lives but who also claim to be persons of faith seeking to follow Jesus, the temptation toward idolatry is strong. It is very tempting and easy to turn the radical challenge of the gospel into something that aligns nicely with the commitments and perspectives that are most natural to me and that fit the lifestyle to which I have become accustomed. Costly grace morphs into cheap grace almost without noticing. As Bowler writes,

> *We are much more likely to do exactly what the Israelites have done: not to have a false image of a false God, but a false image of the true God. We take great comfort in our own version of God instead . . . "Oh, is that an idol? It looked so familiar I would hardly have noticed."*

Or to put it more bluntly and to relate the above to the matters of Holy Week, "My sense is that we are more likely to be Judas than Peter. Peter denies God. Judas betrays him."

I don't know about you, but in my religious tradition and upbringing Judas was a traitor and a scoundrel, while Peter was the alpha disciple who under pressure had a moment of extreme weakness—and who hasn't been there? But Bowler's point is both insightful and disturbing. As a person steeped in the Christian faith ever since I was born, I am unlikely to deny the reality of God in my life. I am far more likely to adjust my beliefs concerning God into what is most comfortable and what fits my current agendas.

Many dramatic treatments of the Passion story speculate that Judas thought he was actually still being a faithful follower of Jesus by forcing Jesus's hand and putting him in front of the authorities. It all went horribly wrong, but perhaps his heart was in the right place. It is much easier and much more naturally human to creatively adjust one's beliefs to one's preferences (Judas) than to turn one's back on one's beliefs altogether (Peter). As Kate Bowler writes, "We are not apostates. We're idolaters . . . After all, what is idolatry except beautiful things that do not transform us?"

It is so easy to be a person of discount faith, to inhabit cheap rather than costly grace. We are unlikely to commit the more dramatic sins. Rather, we are more likely to live comforting pseudo-lives of faith, replacing the most rigorous demands of faith with the best of what we are already doing. The temptation of Judas is far more attractive than the temptation of Peter.

For reflection: What are the ways in which we turn faith into a commodity that is affordable rather than something that demands everything? What are the ways in which we regularly turn the demands of walking with Jesus into something comfortable and manageable?

Maundy Thursday: "Could you not keep awake one hour?"

Years A, B, C: John 13:1–17, 31–35

The drama from Thursday into early Friday of Holy Week is both familiar and inescapable. The Last Supper. The Garden of Gethsemane. Judas's betrayal. Peter's denial. All inexorably leading to trial, conviction, and crucifixion. The elements of the story are so familiar to Christians and others that it is tempting to suppose that there are no more fresh takes or new perspectives to consider on this important but well-worn story.

The lectionary Maundy Thursday gospel continues with John's account of Jesus's last supper with his disciples. But, of course, a lot more happens after that last supper. Jesus heads to the Garden of Gethsemane for some one-on-one conversation with his father, while the disciples tag along. He wants to be alone and asks them to stay and wait for him as he walks on a bit further. Jesus's distress and agony as well as his fear of what is to come are palpable and are understandably the focus of most discussions of this part of the Holy Week drama.

A less discussed, but equally important, detail is that the disciples fall asleep. They literally cannot keep their eyes open. On three different occasions, Jesus returns to them and finds them catching some Zs. Over more than three decades of teaching, many of my students have shown a remarkable ability to fall asleep at the most inopportune times—it's a common human tendency. The disciples have just had dinner, it's getting late, they have nothing to do while Jesus is off praying; no wonder they doze off.

The gospel accounts are very "high church" sounding, but Jesus is clearly annoyed when he finds them asleep.

> *DUDES! Really?? I'm over here literally sweating drops of blood, I've never been so scared and afraid, and you're ASLEEP?? Wake the hell up! Can't you at least do that much?*

I'm sure their collective reaction was something like anyone caught sleeping at the time when they should be awake and alert would have been. "Whaa? Oh! I'm not sleeping, I'm just resting my eyes! Sorry, man! James! Andrew! I can't believe you guys fell asleep! It won't happen again, bro!" But it does—three times.

On the few occasions I have heard this situation discussed, the focus is always on the disciples, so human, so weak, or so disinterested that they fall asleep at the switch. I'm more interested in Jesus's reaction. He hasn't asked the disciples to do anything for him; he doesn't even want them close by. So why is he so upset to find them sleeping? What's the difference between doing nothing and being asleep? In one of his letters to Eberhard Bethge from Tegel prison, Dietrich Bonhoeffer uses this little scene to illustrate a profound insight.

> *Jesus asked in Gethsemane, "Could you not watch with me one hour?" That is a reversal of what the religious person expects from God. We are summoned to share in God's sufferings at the hands of a godless world.*

We expect God to do stuff, to solve problems, to kick butt and take names, but *this* God is not any of that. The only way this God can be in the world is to experience everything it has to offer, to suffer the worst it can do. The least that the disciples can do is be there, to pay attention, to be in solidarity with this man whom they love, whom they have followed, and whom they absolutely do not understand. Jesus feels alone and abandoned by everyone and everything; finding the disciples asleep simply confirms that what he is feeling is the truth.

What would it mean to watch and not fall asleep, to share in God's sufferings? Where exactly is God suffering in our world? Everywhere that a human being has a need of any sort, God is in the middle of it. There is so much suffering that it can be overwhelming. No one of us, not even any one group of us, no matter how well-meaning, can make a significant dent. But Jesus isn't asking the disciples to do anything other than to be aware, to be attentive, and not to tune out. If the answer to "what can I do to help?" is "nothing," at least the question was asked. Asking someone to bear the weight of the world alone is asking a lot—even of God.

For reflection: Simone Weil writes that "[t]he extreme greatness of Christianity lies in the fact that it does not seek a supernatural remedy for suffering but a supernatural use for it." Consider her insight in light of the events of Holy Week.

Good Friday: "Actually, he died"

Years A, B, C: John 18:1–19:42

The gospel reading for the Good Friday liturgy from John's gospel begins with Jesus's arrest in the Garden of Gethsemane and ends with Joseph of Arimathea and Nicodemus preparing Jesus's body for burial and placing it in a tomb. Many Christmas Eves ago, Jeanne, our youngest son Justin, and I were invited to share dinner with a friend from work and her family, which included two precocious and very active children. On display was a beautiful crèche that contained all sorts of interesting items, including a duck and an elephant of roughly the same size. Our friend's five-year-old daughter introduced Justin to the various characters in a monologue interrupted only by a few confirming comments. "And these are some shepherds, those are goats and sheep, that's a dog a turkey and a cow, these are some angels, and that's the baby Jesus." "Oh, really?" "Yes. Actually, he died."

The idea of a suffering and dying God is not new—there are many traditions older than Christianity that include myths and stories of a divinity suffering and dying for various reasons. But this story is so intimately personal, so representative of the crushed hopes and dreams, the inescapable pain and suffering that are fundamentally part of the human experience. Jesus seemed to be something different but turned out to be the same as everyone else: human, limited, subject to suffocating power and injustice, to the random events that ultimately shape each of our stories.

In the religious tradition of my youth, our theology was what scholars call a "theology of glory," one that emphasizes the power and glory of God as exemplified through Christ's sacrifice for the sins of the world on Good Friday and his triumphant resurrection from the dead three days later. It is difficult to pay more than twenty-four hours of attention to the suffering and agony of the cross when you know that it all ends up in the right place. But what happens if the focus of one's Christian faith is Good Friday rather than Easter? What is the difference between a "theology of the cross" and a "theology of glory"?

The Crucifixion without anticipating the Resurrection first moves our attention away from glory, power, and triumph, instead focusing us on suffering, pain, and weakness. This brings home the fundamental fact of Christian belief—God became human, with an emphasis on the human part—something that a theology of glory tends to de-emphasize. A few years ago I had a discussion with my monthly after-church adult education seminar group about the end of the Book of Job in the Jewish

Scriptures, an ending that scholars say was tacked on long after the main story had been written, in which after more than forty chapters of suffering Job gets back everything that he had lost.

I asked the group why someone might have added this "happily ever after" ending to such a dark and human story. "Because the original ending is too tough," someone suggested. "Because people want to believe that suffering has a point, that it is all *for* something," another contributed. "Which makes the better story?" I asked. "The original is truer," an eighty-something regular participant said. "People don't come back. Things that you lose don't return." A theology that relies on a triumphant, happy ending is one that runs the risk of failing to address the human condition as we find it.

In contrast to a theology of glory, in a theology of the cross God addresses the human condition, not by overcoming it, but by becoming part of it. The divine is incarnated in human flesh and thus becomes subject to everything that human beings are subject to—including suffering and death. The Incarnation and the Crucifixion focus our attention on unlimited love, something that we often are too quick to move past in our rush to a happy ending. Good Friday reminds us that because of divine love, the incarnated God did not seek to avoid this fundamental human experience.

Paul argues that the focal point of the Christian faith is the Resurrection: "If Christ be not raised, your faith is vain." More foundationally, however, the Christian faith is vain if there is no cross, no suffering and death of the divine mediator between God and humanity. Only when we see, as did the penitent thief, that this criminal hanging on a cross, rejected and despised by all, is the perfectly just God-human paying the ultimate sacrifice to achieve mediation between God and humanity will we begin to truly experience the mystery of the Christian faith.

If the story ended with Jesus executed as a criminal and dead in a tomb, we still would have reason to believe in a God of love.

The story of a God who becomes fully human, who lives a real human life subject to all things each human being is subject to, including suffering, pain, loss, tragedy, injustice, and death, serves to drive the point deeper. Good Friday reveals just how far the divine chooses to go with us—into the depths of despair and death. I once saw a poster with a dark twist on a familiar saying. "It is always darkest just before—it goes pitch black." And God is there.

For reflection: Centuries of theological debate have centered on where one should focus one's attention most strongly among the events of Holy Week. Which is more meaningful to your faith journey—Jesus's death on the cross or Jesus's resurrection three days later?

Holy Saturday: "Mortals die, and are laid low."

Years A, B, C: Job 14:1–14

Holy Saturday reminds us that we are mortal and that we all will die. Quoting the Book of Job, the Holy Saturday liturgy reminds us that

> [m]ortals die, and are laid low . . . As waters fail from a lake, and a river wastes away and dries up, so mortals lie down and do not rise again; until the heavens are no more, they will not awake or be roused out of their sleep.

Those who loved and followed Jesus, both those who fled and those who stayed, could not have escaped these truths on the day after Jesus was crucified and laid in the tomb. As poet Christian Wiman notes, "resurrection is a fiction and a distraction to anyone who refuses to face the reality of death." Human beings die and are laid low. And Jesus was a human being.

In 1521, the German master Hans Holbein the Younger painted "The Body of the Dead Christ in the Tomb," a work that continues to startle and disturb viewers five hundred years later. Emaciated, battered, unflinchingly grotesque, this figure is in the early stages of putrefaction, of rigor mortis, the glassy eyes and mouth open. Three wounds of the Crucifixion are visible: on the side, the effect of a Roman lance, and nail piercings on the feet and on the hand.

Fyodor Dostoevsky viewed the painting in 1867. His reaction was so intense that his wife became concerned. She reported that he turned white and refused to leave. She dragged him away afraid that his heightened emotions might trigger an epileptic episode. He later remarked, "Such a picture might make one lose one's faith." A character in Dostoevsky's 1868 novel *The Idiot* has the following reaction to a print of Holbein's painting, undoubtedly reflecting Dostoevsky's own reaction a year or so earlier:

> *Supposing that the disciples, the future apostles, the women who had followed Him and stood by the cross, all of whom believed in and worshipped Him—supposing that they saw this tortured body, this face so mangled and bleeding and bruised (and they must have so seen it)—how could they have gazed upon the dreadful sight and yet have believed that He would rise again?*

The most likely answer is that they couldn't. And they didn't. There is no indication in the Gospels that, despite various things that Jesus had said in the previous months, anyone really believed that he was anything but dead for good.

It is clear throughout his novels that Dostoevsky considered confronting doubts to be a central part of faith. He believed that faith wasn't bolstered by finding evidence for God, but rather by believing despite the evidence against the story. That helps explain Dostoevsky's response to Holbein's painting. The depiction of the dead Christ is so realistic, so jarring, that it is a challenge to one's faith to continue to believe in the Resurrection. Our eyes and our experience with death tell us that death is final, there can be no reversal of death to life. Mortals die and are laid low.

The eighteenth-century essayist and philosopher Voltaire once provocatively wrote, "If God did not exist, it would be necessary to invent him." This statement shook up a number of Voltaire's contemporaries, leading many to imagine that any person who could write such a thing seriously must be an atheist. The statement remains provocative, and it is clear from his body of work that whatever Voltaire might have been, he was not a traditional religious believer. But with the apparent meaninglessness of human existence and reality in view, Voltaire's famous claim is absolutely true. The darkest and most sobering parts of human reality cry out for, actually demand, a response. The human epitaph cannot be "Life's a bitch, and then you die."

All sorts of responses to whether life has meaning without belief in something greater than us, ranging from religious through philosophical and literary to political, have been offered over the centuries, responses that often conflict with each other and even more frequently fail to take the fundamental problem on squarely. Which of these responses is true? More importantly, how can we know if *any* of them are true? How can we be sure that they are anything more than a collection of tunes human beings have written to whistle in the dark until the night overwhelms them?

We cannot be sure. Yet billions of people have been and continue to be willing to shape their lives, to stake their very existence, on the truth of one or more of these stories. Why? Because there is something in the human heart that has to believe them, something that has to hope. And it is that very longing and hope that is perhaps most convincing. As Simone

Weil reminds us, "[I]f we ask our Father for bread, he will not give us a stone."

The third and final portion of George Friedrich Handel's masterpiece *Messiah*, immediately following the "Hallelujah Chorus," begins with "I Know That My Redeemer Liveth," a soaring, beautiful soprano solo setting of a text from Job, with a concluding sentiment from 1 Corinthians:

> *I know that my redeemer liveth, and that he shall stand at the latter day upon the earth;*
> *And though worms destroy this body, yet in my flesh shall I see God.*
> *For now is Christ risen from the dead, the first fruits of them that sleep.*

From the depths of despair, literally from the middle of a pile of ashes, Job clings to a hopeful story, that there is a transcendent and triumphant divine response to human incapacity, despair, and hopelessness. It's a wonderful story. How can we not believe it?

For reflection: Kathleen Norris writes that "a myth is a story that you know must be true the first time you hear it." Do the seminal stories of the Christian faith present truths that transcend the facts of what might or might not have actually happened?

CHAPTER 6

Easter—Everything Has Changed

Easter season is fifty days long, running from Easter to Pentecost. In the Christian liturgical year, it doesn't get any bigger than Easter. The Easter season is packed with spectacular events—an empty tomb, the ascension, Pentecost—more than enough, one might imagine, to keep one energized spiritually for some time. Easter is the celebration of the promise of hope, the promise of new life, that surely after darkness there is light, and that within the deepest betrayals lie the possibilities of forgiveness.

Yet as author Barbara Johnson writes, "[W]e are Easter people living in a Good Friday world," a world that provides more Good Friday moments on a daily basis. Eventually, the joy of Easter and what follows in its wake fades. What then? The lectionary texts for Easter Sunday and the Easter season that follows hit all of the familiar highs but do not flinch from placing them in the context of fear, danger, betrayal, and unbelief. As Kate Bowler writes, "[T]there is no cure for being human"—the Easter season explores what happens when the highest of highs meets the reality of daily existence.

Easter: Now it begins

Year A, B, C: John 20:1–18; A: Matthew 28:1–10; B: Mark 16:1–8; C: Luke 24:1–12

The lectionary gospel readings for Easter Sunday are from John's gospel, with an alternative available from one of the Synoptic Gospels in each year. As is often the case, each gospel account differs both in details and timeline. Rather than getting hung up on facts and details—none of which we can know with certainty two millennia after the fact—it is important to remember the difference between faith and fact. Although *something* happened on Easter morning, faith is not dependent on any particular detail being true. Faith is expressed not in certainty about details, but rather in how one lives out the deeper meanings of the story.

When she was a puppy, our corgi Bovina developed a routine for greeting the sun as it peeked its head over our backyard privacy fence each morning. The first morning rays reflect off our back storm door; if someone moves the door back and forth, the reflection moves along the side and back fence. Everyone rises before the sun gets up at our house—Bovina immediately insists on going into the backyard and occasionally barking until the sun rises, then barking even more until an accommodating parent moves the door so she can joyously and noisily chase the reflection. Even as a young adult a couple of years later, Bovina still waits patiently to greet the dawn every morning, even though the new house built in the empty lot behind us now blocks the rising sun's rays from shining on our back door. She gives new meaning to "I will sing and make melody ... I will awake the dawn" from Psalm 57.

Bovina's routine reminds me of my family's "Sunrise Service" routine every Easter morning during my youth. The heartier members of our small Baptist church would gather a half hour or so before sunrise at the home of a family whose house was on a ridge overlooking our Vermont town's valley. Looking east across the valley from their backyard, I could see the two ski areas where I had spent every free winter moment over the past months, even when the temperature was well below zero.

As sunrise approached, the pastor would read from one of the gospel accounts of early Easter morning, seeking to hit "Why do you seek the living among the dead?" or "Woman, why are you weeping?" depending on the gospel being read, just as the sun peeked its head over Burke Mountain. Of course, there were some Easters when it was raining, and I remember at least one when it was snowing—on those occasions we did our business in the living room looking out the glass doors and windows toward the east. We were all hardy New Englanders, but hardiness has its limits.

I am a morning person, so I'll take sunrise over sunset any day. I've experienced many sunrises over the years walking onto my college's beautiful campus headed east to my office or the gym. But the most memorable sunrise I ever experienced was in my early teens when my father, my older brother, and I visited the Grand Canyon. From one of the South Rim points, we gathered with a few dozen other folks to await the dawn. There was no sound other than the breeze.

Until, that is, a three- or four-year-old ran screaming through the group delighted by something or other. "SSSSIIIHHHH!" the child's parents and everyone else immediately said, just as they would probably have done if the kid had run up and down an aisle in church making the same racket. The sunrise a few minutes later was a sacred event—we were all standing on holy ground.

I like the Psalmist's claim that "I will awake the dawn." It implies that the dawn is more than just a product of physical laws and forces—we have something to do with it. Of course, the sun rises every morning whether anyone is watching or not, but we have the capacity to participate in its meaning and value. Certainly the stories of those who encountered an empty tomb, then experienced the resurrected Jesus on that first Easter morning make the empty tomb that much more poignant and sacred. The family, friends, and followers of Jesus had thought everything was over. But as Zerah in *Jesus of Nazareth* says when looking into the empty tomb, "Now it begins."

It is easy to forget the pain and suffering that led to the Resurrection. It is also easy to overlook that each of the Gospel Easter accounts report that the initial reactions of those who first saw the empty tomb included both confusion and terror. Pain, suffering, death, fear, and uncertainty remain parts of human experience and reality. And yet . . . everything has changed.

For reflection: Imagine that you were one of the first to find the stone at Jesus's tomb rolled away and the tomb empty on that first Easter morning. Be honest—what would your reaction have been?

Easter: Getting Jesus out of the tomb

During a recent Easter Sunday sermon, the homilist told the story of Gladys, a life-long pillar of her Congregational church, one of only three churches within a seventy-mile radius in her area of the rural Midwest; the other two were Lutheran and Roman Catholic. One fateful Easter morning, Gladys arrived with her three children in tow, ready for Easter festivities.

The homily was given by a young man who, according to Gladys, was "too smart for his own good." The elements the sermon wove together included spring, new life, and baby rabbits, but virtually nothing was said about Jesus or the Resurrection. That was Gladys's last time at the Congregational church; starting the next Sunday she and her family joined forces with the Lutherans down the road, a church where, according to Gladys, "they at least knew how to get Jesus out of the tomb!"

So how do we who profess the Christian faith get Jesus out of the tomb and keep him out, two millennia after the supposed historical event celebrated every Easter? Because, after all, Gladys's complaints about the Congregational preacher notwithstanding, Easter is about more than the fact that Jesus reportedly walked out of the tomb he had been in for three days. It is about transformation, new life, and how to live that new life on a daily basis. It's an affirmation of God's love for humanity, a statement that all are invited into relationship with the divine.

New Testament scholar N. T. Wright made this provocative observation in a recent book concerning the stories of the day:

> *The practical, theological, spiritual, ethical, pastoral, political, missionary, and hermeneutical implications of the mission and message of Jesus differ radically depending upon what one believes happened at Easter.*

Indeed they do—but beyond confirming that the Easter story is true in the sense that "these stories are true—and some of them actually happened," debates concerning the historical veracity of the foundational stories of Christianity often deflect our attention from what is at the heart of the Easter story.

New life arrives in ways both surprising and inexplicable. I don't know what all of the dozens of little green things that sprout up throughout my backyard and flower beds every spring are, but they are alive. I don't know what the little downy woodpecker hammering away on the vinyl siding of our neighbor's house one early spring morning was thinking, but it was life in action. Christians often try to make the Easter story more manageable by seeking to insert certainty where open-endedness and wonder are more appropriate, often with regrettable results.

In an Easter interview with CNN a few years ago, Barbara Brown Taylor spoke about various ways in which our attempts to control mystery can go badly. Taylor is a writer and speaker in great demand, partly because she regularly "says things that you aren't supposed to say," including writing about the dark side of faith, leaving the Episcopal priesthood because of a faith crisis, and discussing what every person of faith can and should learn from religious traditions other than her or his own.

Writing and speaking about such questions and topics have, not surprisingly, attracted both high praise and severe criticism. The sharpest criticism has, sadly, come from a certain type of Christian, people Taylor calls "true believers":

> *True believers are among the meanest people I've ever met. I cannot think of anybody of another faith who has wounded me like Christians. Judged, condemned to hell, cast out of the body of the faithful—look me up online.*

I grew up in a religious world in which this sort of toxicity was always just below the surface. This brand of Christianity gives the faith a bad name; indeed, for many people, both insiders and outsiders, this *is* Christianity. Doing damage in the name of the Christian faith serves to undermine the message of Easter by showing that the new life and growth promised by the Resurrection is simply a thin veneer over judgment and fear. True believers don't really want Jesus out of the tomb. They want him to stay buried where he can be controlled.

Toward the end of the CNN interview, Barbara Brown Taylor was asked what, after decades of grappling with the Christian faith, Easter means to her today. Her response is one that people from all faith traditions or none at all can resonate with. Here's how we get Jesus out of the tomb and keep him out:

> *These days I would say Easter is the eruption of life from a tomb as God's huge surprise, going in a different direction, and if anything, proof that you can never predict how God is going to act next . . . Now I value Easter as the reminder that you never know where life is going to come from next, and there's no sense being attached to the day before yesterday because the day before yesterday is dead, and today something is alive.*

For reflection: If you were to describe what Easter means to you to a friend who does not share your Christian faith, what would you say?

Second Sunday of Easter: A doubting disciple

Years A, B, C: John 20:19–31

The Second Sunday of Easter is "Doubting Thomas" Sunday, focusing on the story of Jesus's disciple Thomas shortly after the Resurrection. He was absent when the risen Jesus appeared to his fellow disciples for the first time and refused to believe their report. I was taught in my youth that Thomas was a loser because he would not believe reports of Jesus's resurrection until he had seen and handled the man himself. But over the years, Thomas has become one of my spiritual heroes, and doubt has become one of my favorite virtues.

Consider another of history's great skeptics and doubters. Michel de Montaigne's world was filled with religious fervor and piety, as well as hatred and violence. Sixteenth-century France was not a pretty place—in the wake of the Protestant Reformation, Christians were killing each other with regularity and abandon, all in the name of Christ. Catholics and Protestants each were certain that they were right; energized by such certainty, each was willing to kill the other in the name of truth and right belief.

Michel was an upper-class landowner and occasional politician and diplomat. Sensitive and melancholy by nature, Montaigne was appalled by the violence that was tearing his country, his town, his neighborhood, even his own family apart. Accordingly, he did what any introverted, sensitive, melancholy guy would have done. He withdrew to his turret library in the small castle on his family estate and wrote—for the rest of his life.

Reflecting on the world in which he lived, Montaigne writes that "there is no hostility so extreme as that of the Christian. Our zeal works marvels when it seconds our inclination toward hatred, cruelty, ambition, greed, slander, and rebellion." Michel's antidote? Let's stop claiming to be certain about what we believe and try some healthy doubt and skepticism on for size. Certainty is vastly overrated and is frequently dangerous, especially when claimed concerning matters that are far beyond the reach of human capacities. For the most part, human beings are not designed for the rarified air of certainty. Montaigne directly challenges those who "claim to know the frontiers and bounds of the will of God," observing that "there is nothing in the whole world madder than bringing matters down to the measure of our own capacities."

Human beings claiming certainty about the will and nature of God would be humorous, and Montaigne often presents it that way, were it not that such claims are often the basis for the worst of what human beings are capable of, including prejudice, violence, and killing. Even as we seek preposterously to elevate ourselves to the level of the divine, Montaigne reminds us that we remain rooted in our humanity. "There is no use our mounting on stilts, for on stilts we must still walk on our own legs. And on the loftiest throne in the world we are still sitting only on our own ass."

Because of his willingness to embrace messiness and uncertainty as part of the human condition, Montaigne is one of my heroes. And so is Thomas. He was always brought to our attention in Sunday School as someone not to be like; indeed, Jesus's put-down of Thomas after Thomas finally believes— "Blessed are those who have not seen and yet have come to believe"—provides us two thousand years later with something to be proud of.

But there is another way to read this account, a way in which Thomas turns out not to be a spiritual weakling but rather to be a model of how to approach the spiritual life. We don't know much about Thomas apart from this story. He is included in the lists of disciples in the first three Gospels, but John is the only gospel in which Thomas makes an actual appearance. He apparently is not one of the inner circle, but he occasionally makes appropriate comments and asks good questions.

In the Easter 2 gospel reading from John, we find the disciples, minus Thomas, hiding in a room with the doors locked. Peter and John have already seen the empty tomb, but there is an atmosphere of confusion, uncertainty, and fear in the room. Suddenly Jesus appears to them, and all uncertainty vanishes. But Thomas was not there. When the other disciples report that "we have seen the Lord," Thomas's response places him forever in the disciples' hall of shame: "Unless I see the mark of the nails in his hands and put my finger in the mark of the nails and my hand in his side, I will not believe."

Remember that the other disciples apparently did not believe until Jesus appeared to them. Why should Thomas not be cut the same slack? Embedded in the middle of this story is a fundamental truth: A true encounter with the divine is never second-hand. Hearing about someone else's experiences, trying to find God through the haze of various religious and doctrinal filters, is not a replacement for the real thing.

Doubt and uncertainty are central threads in the human fabric; both play a fundamental role in belief. As Pulitzer Prize-winning author Annie Dillard writes, "Doubt and dedication often go hand in hand." Unfounded claims of certainty undermine this. Don't believe on the cheap. Better to remain uncertain and in doubt one's whole life, doggedly tracking what glimmers of light one sees, than to settle for a cheap knock-off or a counterfeit.

For reflection: Partially in response to Montaigne's embrace of doubt, René Descartes one generation later argued that something is true only if it is indubitable and cannot possibly be false. Which of these perspectives do you find most relevant to your faith journey—Montaigne's or Descartes's?

Third Sunday of Easter: "We had hoped"

Year A: Luke 24:13–35

"Now faith, hope, and love abide ... and the greatest of these is love." These words from the apostle Paul are heard at many, perhaps most, weddings. Everyone wants to believe that love is the greatest, especially on their wedding day. Faith is part of my DNA—challenging it, trying to get rid of it, redefining it, being confused by it, and generally struggling with the "f-word" (as I call it in the classroom) has shaped me for as long as I can remember. I'm not so sure about hope.

Several years ago, I asked Jeanne what she thought the opposite of faith is. She first answered "despair," then immediately took it back and said, "I guess despair's the opposite of hope." After a quick check on Google, I found that she was right (again). The immediate etymological root of "despair" is the Old French *despoir*: hopelessness. So, what is hope?

Although Easter is certainly about love and faith, it is arguably mostly about hope. There is no shortage of material to consider during the Easter season—the empty tomb, Peter and John racing to take a look, the authorities scrambling to explain what happened, the poignant exchange between Mary Magdalene and Jesus. But my personal favorite Easter-related story is the Easter 3 Year A gospel—Luke's account of two disciples on the road to Emmaus. It's such a human story—the bitter sadness and devastation of Cleopas and his unnamed companion (call him Bob) is palpable.

The usual take on the story is that Jesus is risen and walking with Cleopas and Bob, but they are either too dense or blinded by tears to know it's him. Jesus gives them a free and unsolicited theology lesson; as soon as they recognize him after he breaks the bread at dinner he vanishes. Three words are particularly resonant: "*We had hoped* that he was the one to redeem Israel." We had hoped. And our hope was in vain.

Hope is a tough nut to crack. Every human life is marked by "we had hoped" moments that we never quite get over. I hoped that I would become a concert pianist. Jeanne hoped she would marry someone who could dance. But the dashed hopes of Cleopas and Bob are far more crushing. It's easy to criticize Cleopas and Bob for failing to recognize that what they had hoped for was walking with them for seven miles, but that's not entirely fair.

True, Jesus does "redeem Israel," and everybody else for that matter, but the redemption Cleopas, Bob, and others were hoping for was a political redemption and establishment of an earthly kingdom by the Messiah. And it's very telling that the Jesus-guided tour through the Jewish Scriptures touching on prophetic texts indicating that the Messiah would suffer and die doesn't do anything for Cleopas and Bob. It's not until the three of them have a meal, a human experience rather than a classroom experience, that they see it's been Jesus all the time.

This is where the story usually ends, but it gets even more interesting. Cleopas and Bob run back to Jerusalem and report to the disciples what happened; in the middle of their story, Jesus reappears. And in another human, all-too-human moment—Cleopas, Bob, the eleven disciples, and everyone else is scared out of their wits. They think he's a ghost. It's not until Jesus lets them check out his body with its scars, as he invited Thomas to do in the previous Sunday's gospel, and eats a piece of fish in front of them that they realize it's really him. The whole story is fraught with humor, fallibility, and humanity.

In *Amazing Grace*, Kathleen Norris asks, "Does it ever surprise you that God chooses to be revealed in so fallible a fashion?" Yes, it does. All the time. Even when our greatest hopes are satisfied, it's always in some sideways, back door, behind the scenes, fuzzy, and oblique sort of way. And that can be frustrating. Jesus's resurrection, the most spectacular and crucial event in human history, is surrounded by so many instances of mistaken identity, fumbling around, uncertainty, and missteps that it is truly comical.

But it makes perfect sense and brings the central pillars of the Christian faith—the Incarnation, the Crucifixion, and the Resurrection—together. The whole idea of Incarnation, of God becoming human through and through, is outrageous and ludicrous at its core. What self-respecting creator of the universe would do it this way? Only one that loves what was created so much that becoming part of it, miraculously, is not a step down but is actually the only way to accomplish what has to be accomplished. We know that we are flawed, incomplete, jumbled, and messed-up creatures, so why should we be surprised that our hopes get addressed in that way?

The divinely infused cycle of death and resurrection is around us everywhere, in nature coming alive after a long winter, in church services populated by octogenarians and infants, in the annual arrival of new late teens ready to be taught on campus, just to name a few examples from my own daily life. It is not at all surprising that the resurrected Jesus, the hope of the world, was revealed in the midst of the daily and mundane rather than in power and glory. Kathleen Norris once again: "In a religion based on a human incarnation of the divine, when ideology battles experience, it is fallible, ordinary experience that must win."

For reflection: In **Downton Abbey**, *the dowager countess Violet says that "hope is a tease to prevent us from accepting reality." How would you respond?*

Fourth Sunday of Easter:
The good shepherd

Year B: Psalm 23; John 10:11–16

Easter 4 is known as "Good Shepherd Sunday." The assigned Gospels for years A, B, and C take us consecutively through the first half of John 10, where Jesus says, "I am the good shepherd. The good shepherd lays down his life for the sheep." Psalm 23, perhaps the most familiar of all psalms, is part of the assigned readings for all three years. Psalm 23 tells us that the Lord our shepherd leads us in paths of righteousness and even is with us in our darkest hours, as we walk through the valley of the shadow of death, while one of Matthew's parables is about a tender-hearted shepherd who leaves ninety-nine sheep safely penned up in order to find a lost one so he can restore his flock to an even hundred.

As a youngster, I always bristled at the frequent biblical comparison of human beings to sheep, because I knew (or had read at least) that sheep are both smelly and stupid. Although artists' renditions of Jesus with sheep are always lovely and peaceful, it is not a compliment when a group of people are referred to as a "flock" or as a bunch of sheep. "Sheeple" has become a typical epithet to aim at those whom one suspects are followers with little independent thought. I still resist the analogy. According to my youngest son, who was a vet tech for several years, goats—as well as just about every other animal—are much more interesting and smarter than sheep. I would prefer to be compared to just about any other animal than a sheep.

During a memorable ten-day vacation in Scotland a few summers ago, I conservatively estimate that Jeanne and I saw about seven billion sheep. They were everywhere, including across the road from two of the B and B's we stayed in, as well as along the side of (and sometimes in the middle of) virtually every road that we drove on the wrong side of. Interestingly, I don't recall that we ever saw a shepherd. When I asked someone about this, she seemed surprised by the idea that sheep might need constant shepherding. Most of the sheep Jeanne and I saw had a mark for identification purposes—these "brands" looked as if they had been spray painted on the unfortunate animal. Sheep in Scotland are clearly for wool growing, not eating. I don't remember seeing mutton or lamb chops on the menu at any of the restaurants we visited.

We learned a few important things about sheep while in Scotland, things worth keeping in mind if we want the God-is-shepherd-and-we-are-sheep metaphor to work. Sheep are tough and resilient. A shepherd can stick his or her sheep out in a pasture with sufficient grass, mark them as his or her own, then walk away—apparently for days or weeks at a time. Sheep don't need constant pampering and attention. They are naturally equipped to survive all sorts of weather, all the time slowly but surely growing the wool that is, after all, the primary purpose of their existence.

If God is the shepherd and we are the sheep, we can expect to be left alone and to have to rely on our own devices for long stretches of time. But the slow work of growth and productivity continues reliably whether the divine shepherd is in the pasture or not. As the sheep of God's flock, we are naturally designed to be useful and productive in all sorts of ways, no matter what the circumstances are, and regardless of whether it seems as if nothing is happening and that the shepherd has left for good. The shepherd knows that we are tougher than we think we are, and that we are a lot more valuable than we might appear. And when the storms come, as they always will, the shepherd knows that we can handle that as well.

And yet there's another, equally important side to the story. One of the most beloved verses in Psalm 23 says, "Even though I walk through the darkest valley, I fear no evil; for you are with me." I learned recently that in the original language, the last passage simply says, "you me." The shepherd is not *with* the sheep—the shepherd and the sheep are *one*.

For reflection: Human beings are often likened to sheep in both the Jewish Scriptures and the New Testament. The cultures in which these books were written were fully aware of the dynamics between shepherds and their sheep, but most of us are not. To what extent are these stories relevant to twenty-first-century people of faith?

Fifth Sunday of Easter: When the rules change

Year C: Acts 11:1–18

During the Easter season, a reading from the book of Acts often replaces the first reading from the Jewish Scriptures. Acts is about the early Jesus communities and the spread of the "good news" inexorably from Palestine toward Rome and beyond. The Easter 5 Year C reading from Acts is an important and strange story that, in many ways, serves as one of the pivot points in the early Jesus communities' understanding of what it meant to be a follower of Jesus.

Often lost two thousand years after the fact is just how disorienting all of this must have been. Major debates raged about exactly what this new set of beliefs was. Was it a new version of Judaism? If so, then new Jesus followers should be subject to the same dietary and behavioral rules from the Torah that all Jews were subject to; male converts, for instance, should be circumcised.

Or was this set of beliefs something new altogether, perhaps a challenge and direct threat to Judaism? Complicating the issue, at least according to evidence from the Gospels, is that Jesus himself was not always clear or consistent about who his message and teaching was for. Jesus was a Jew, and at times clearly said that his message was for the "house of Israel," while at other times he packaged it for everyone, including non-Jews.

In Acts 10 we find Peter, the man who perhaps knew Jesus best and who, as the alpha disciple, is now at the forefront of spreading the good news, hungry and exhausted after an extended prayer session on the rooftop of a friend's house in Joppa, where he is staying. And then the strangest thing happens, as Peter reports to some critics in Acts 11:

> *In a trance I saw a vision. There was something like a large sheet coming down from heaven, being lowered by its four corners; and it came close to me. As I looked at it closely I saw four-footed animals, beasts of prey, reptiles, and birds of the air. I also heard a voice saying to me, "Get up, Peter; kill and eat."*

The sheet is full of all sorts of animals that, according to Jewish law, must not be eaten under any circumstances, as Peter immediately recognizes.

> *But I replied, "By no means, Lord; for nothing profane or unclean has ever entered my mouth."*

Peter knows the rules backward and forward; furthermore, he knows that for a Jew, strict obedience to these rules is required in order to be in right relationship both with God and with one's community.

But as seems to happen so often in the context of what we think we know about God and our relationship with the divine, the rule book is thrown out entirely.

> *But a second time the voice answered from heaven, "What God has made clean, you must not call profane."*

Imagine Peter's consternation and confusion. Imagine the consternation and confusion of his fellow Jewish believers when they find out that he has been hanging out with and spreading the good news to Gentiles. For after the voice from heaven in essence tells Peter, "You know all of that stuff in the Torah about what not to eat in order to be in the right relationship with God, the stuff that has defined the diet of a faithful Jew for the past couple of millennia? Never mind. You can eat anything you want," Peter is further informed that the human equivalent of unclean animals—the Gentiles—are now to be recipients of the good news that you might have mistakenly thought was just for Jews.

There's this Roman centurion by the name of Cornelius who has been asking some really good questions—go to his house and help him out. As we learn in Acts 10, Cornelius and his household convert to the message of Jesus, start speaking in tongues as Peter and others did at Pentecost, more conservative Jews are appalled, and eventually there is a big council in Jerusalem to decide what the hell's going on. But Pandora's box has been opened, never to be closed again. The old rule book is out, and it's anyone's guess where this is going to end up.

Don't you hate it when someone changes the rules of the game at the very moment when you've gotten really good at working within the framework of the old rules? Just when you think you have everything relevant and necessary figured out, it all changes. Peter's vision was a challenge to see things differently, to view one's reality with traditional and familiar lenses set to the side and to see with new eyes. If what tradition said was unclean is in fact clean, then everything is being reset. People of faith are, in our own confusing and disorienting time, being asked to see differently, to cast aside categories that are often entrenched, in order to see others as real human beings just as we are.

In certain circles, this is called "evolving faith." We are called to see differently so that the human being in front of us is not dark-skinned, poor, female, gay, disabled, conservative, wealthy,

Muslim, male, straight, ugly, liberal, old, Christian, obese, or attractive, but rather is a person whose needs, hopes, and dreams are real and independent of us. It is a *task* to come to see the world as it is. When I believe that I have seen all there is to see, the Christ in me says, "Let me look again."

For reflection: What are the times in your faith journey when things you thought you knew with certainty turned out to be subject to change?

Sixth Sunday of Easter: "Do you want to be made well?"

Year C: John 5:1–9

One of the gospel choices for Easter 6 Year C is the story in John 5 of the man who has been waiting by the Pool of Bethesda in Jerusalem for thirty-eight years for someone to help him into the healing waters of the pool when they are "stirred up." This story showed up unexpectedly during an oral examination with one of my students not long ago.

I have taught a colloquium called "Grace, Truth, and Freedom in the Nazi Era" five times with a now-retired colleague and friend from the history department; we always conclude the course with thirty-minute oral exams. One time, the conversation took a very interesting turn. An author whom we considered during the semester was Simone Weil, who suggests that attentive listening is the first step to bringing those who are "afflicted," persons whose identity has been stripped from them either by chance or deliberately by others, back toward healing and a restoration of their humanity.

Think of the emaciated, skeletal prisoners of Auschwitz on the day that Allied soldiers liberated the death camp. These are people from whom every shred of dignity, identity, and humanity has been stripped. They are the walking dead. And, to use Simone Weil's word, they are "afflicted." The temptation, of course, is to seek to address the most obvious physical needs of such people—food, clothing, shelter, medical care, and so on. But, Weil suggests, there is something more profound and immediate than physical help that those who are afflicted need. She writes that

> [t]he capacity to give one's attention to a sufferer is a very rare and difficult thing; it is almost a miracle; it is a miracle ... The love of our neighbor in all its fullness simply means being able to say to him: "What are you going through?" It is a recognition that the sufferer exists, not only as a unit in a collection, or a specimen from the social category labeled "unfortunate," but as a man, exactly like us, who was one day stamped with a special mark by affliction.

How do I begin to restore the humanity and dignity of one from whom those things have been violently stripped away? Not by addressing their physical needs as one would solve a mathematical equation, but rather by saying, "tell me your story." In this way I tell the afflicted person—to use a current popular phrase—"I see you. At the core of this starving, filthy, corpse-like creature in front of me I recognize a fellow human being. What are you going through?" And in that way, through the simple but profound recognition of another's personhood, the restoration of human dignity begins.

Many of our colloquium students found Weil's thought challenging, but profound. As my colleague and I conversed with one of our students during her oral exam, the story from John 5 occurred to me. The man in the story has been at the pool for thirty-eight years. After briefly describing the story—which, as it turned out, she was familiar with—I said to my student, "We know that Jesus is going to heal this guy. But instead of just getting down to business, he first asks the strangest question: *Do you want to be made well?* Why does Jesus ask this?"

At first, the student speculated that perhaps this man made his meager living begging as a lame man. Jesus is asking him, "Are you sure you are prepared for the consequences of no longer being lame?" The man won't be able to make money begging if he can walk. But after some further conversation, she suggested rather that perhaps Jesus is exhibiting Simone Weil's attentiveness. By asking for the man's consent, Jesus shows that he does not consider the lame man as a problem to be solved, a disease to be cured, or another opportunity to perform a miracle, but considers him rather as a person, a human being with dignity, whose permission is needed simply because he is a human being equal in dignity to the one who is asking him the question.

The scene is striking in its simplicity. Jesus asks the question because he wants the man to know that, despite his affliction, his poverty, his bitterness, and his pain, Jesus recognizes in him the beauty and dignity of a human being. And Jesus will not presume to invade this man's world without his consent. There is nothing more profound contained in the story of Christianity than that God became human—and that this was not so much a reflection of how far God had to descend, but rather of how infinitely valuable human beings are. As the traditional Hindu greeting "Namaste" says: "That which is holy in me recognizes that which is holy in you."

For reflection: Imagine that the primary message of Jesus is that his followers are to restore personhood and dignity to those who are afflicted. Where would you start, and what would you do?

Ascension Sunday: Passing the baton

Years A, B, and C: Luke 24:50–53; Acts 1:1–11

Ascension Day is forty days after Easter, so it always falls on the Thursday between the sixth and seventh Sunday of Easter.

It is typical to celebrate the Ascension on the seventh Sunday of Easter, the Sunday before Pentecost. The relevant readings are from the first chapter of Acts and the conclusion of Luke's gospel.

A number of years ago, Ascension Sunday happened to be the seventeenth and last Sunday that I would be worshiping at St. Johns Abbey in Collegeville, Minnesota. As I sat in my choir stall seat during seven o'clock morning prayer, then in the sanctuary later in the morning during Mass, there was a certain wistfulness and a bit of emotion, but not as much as I expected. For this Ascension Sunday was an appropriate milestone in my spiritual growth, a marker of the point at which I would tentatively and with fear and trembling take what I had learned and experienced over the previous four months of sabbatical "into all the world."

I was never taught to pay attention to Ascension Sunday in my religious tradition. Even after I was introduced to the liturgical calendar for the first time in my mid-twenties, Ascension Sunday was simply the Sunday before Pentecost. But as I experienced for the first time the psalms and New Testament texts on that Ascension Sunday, I thought, "Wow. Jesus was the ultimately prepared and successful teammate."

A disturbingly common mishap over the years in the summer Olympic games has been the failure of U.S. track and field relay teams. Individually, these teams almost always are made up of the best runners, top to bottom, of any nation's relay contingent. But great individuals do not make a successful relay team make. In a relay race, each runner is required not only to run their lap as swiftly as possible but also to hand the baton to the next runner smoothly and securely within a specified number of meters. As the baton falls to the track during these attempted transfers, time after time, the truth becomes crystal clear.

In the quintessential American spirit, the members of the U.S. relay teams have spent far too much time honing their individual running skills and far too little time practicing how to be a team. Passing a baton while both the passer and passee are running, one decelerating and one accelerating, within a limited amount of space takes practice—practice that is not nearly as sexy or stimulating as running as fast as one can by oneself.

Ascension Sunday completes the story of the Incarnation that began with Jesus's birth. Jesus doesn't ascend out of his human body to heaven—he takes it with him, because the next lap of this story, the "Christ in us" lap, is just about ready to explode. Jesus showed extraordinary patience with his all-too-human followers during his short stay on earth, teaching them basic truths through stories and actions, all preparation for when it would be up to them to receive the baton and run their own incarnational race. The forty days after the Resurrection were all practice for a smooth passing of the baton.

Jesus kept telling them, "It's all right. I'm not leaving you alone. It's better for you that I am leaving because I'll be sending you the greatest teammate ever. You can do this because I'll still be with you. When I leave, don't go crazy and start running in every direction out of fear or impatience. Wait. Pray. You'll know when it's time to run. And when you do, you'll turn the world upside-down." And when the clouds closed on Jesus's heels as he ascended into heaven, for once the men and women who had loved and followed him did what they were told. They went into an upper room in Jerusalem and waited.

I'm told that the receiver of the baton in a relay race should not seek to accelerate until she or he feels the slap of the baton in the palm of the receiving hand they have extended behind them as they begin to run. The receiver never sees the runner coming up behind, but there's no mistaking the transfer from the unseen runner when it happens. And in the upper room, ten days after Jesus left, there was no mistaking that the baton had been successfully transferred.

The Incarnation goes on, and we recipients of the Holy Spirit carry it "to the ends of the earth." In his homily on that Ascension Sunday, the abbot observed that with Ascension Day, the Easter message of "Glory, Glory, Glory" that has been front and center since Easter changes to "Go!" The word to me that day and ever since was, "Take what you've been given, what you've found, and go." As Psalm 19 says,

Day unto day takes up the story
And night unto night makes known the message.

We are carrying the baton and are to run as if our lives depended on it. Because they do.

For reflection: Is faith something private and individual, or does a vibrant faith require community and teamwork? If both, which is more important?

Pentecost: "The rush of a violent wind"

Years A, B, and C: Acts 2:1–21; Year C: Genesis 11:1–9

After Christmas and Easter, Pentecost is arguably the most important day in the liturgical year. The central text for the day is from Acts 2, when the Holy Spirit descended like "the rush of a violent wind." I was taught that Pentecost marks the "birthday of the church," but it signifies something much greater and more important than the start of a church or religion. Pentecost tells us that in the midst of our differences and failures to understand each other, we are united by the presence of the divine within us.

The Year C reading from the Jewish Scriptures for Pentecost is the fascinating story of the Tower of Babel. This story is traditionally interpreted as a tale similar to Noah and the flood a few chapters earlier in Genesis—human beings are getting uppity and God puts them in their place. Because of their hubris,

God scatters people in every direction as well as "confus[ing] the language of all the earth" so they can no longer understand each other. Just as we traditionally blame Adam and Eve for original sin, so our seeming inability to understand or truly communicate with each other is the result of Babel, whose inhabitants thought themselves to be greater than they actually were.

There is no obvious challenge to God from the people of Babel. They simply want to establish a city, share their talents, build a tower as tall as their abilities and technology will allow, settle down, stop wandering, and "make a name for ourselves—otherwise we shall be scattered abroad upon the face of the whole earth." In other words, this is a story about the early beginnings of what we recognize as civilization. Realizing that the world is a demanding and scary place, human beings learn that there is strength and security in cooperation and numbers. Self-reliance and independence are better established collectively than individually. There is no obvious sense of humans thumbing their noses at God here, just a desire to reap the benefits of community. So why is God upset?

From the perspective of Elohim (the plural name for God used in this story), apparently this is a *very* big deal in a negative sense. Something about human attempts at solidarity, independence, and strength is threatening to God throughout the Jewish Scriptures, never more so than in this story. "This is only the beginning of what they will do; nothing that they propose to do will now be impossible for them." These amazing creatures that we made? Look at what they can do! Planning, creativity, cooperation, independence, ambition—the sky's the limit! Not exactly. "Come, let us go down, and confuse their language there, so that they will not understand one another's speech."

At the very least, the Tower of Babel story reveals that human progress by its very nature creates tension with what is greater than us. God is made uneasy by the prospect that the human beings they created might actually have a mind and will of their own. These are the early seeds of tension between the secular and the sacred. The divine response? Put an end to it now. Scatter them, confuse them, cut this thing off at the knees.

There is far more than a simple surface-level connection between the story of Pentecost in Acts 2 and the Tower of Babel story in Genesis 11. In truth, Pentecost undoes Babel, turns it on its head. Rather than dispersing human beings and confusing their language, at Pentecost the divine unites human beings by causing them to understand each other.

Pentecost tells us that the divine is neither angry at nor threatened by us. God wants human beings to cooperate and communicate effectively. Furthermore, our ability to do so is a divine gift. Whenever we overcome the vast differences that separate us, differences too many to count, the divine is present. Whenever human beings connect, not by eliminating differences but rather by finding commonality, enhanced and deepened by our diverse perspectives and experiences, God is there. The divine strategy, culminating in Pentecost, is simple and profound. The distance between God and humanity in Genesis 11 has been breached. Pentecost completes the story of the Incarnation. We all are "God carriers."

Pentecost also tells us that the divine solution to our failure to understand each other is not conformity, getting everyone on the same page and believing the same thing. Those present did not miraculously start speaking the same language at Pentecost, as humans did at the start of the Babel story. At Pentecost, each person retained his or her own language and was divinely enabled to hear the good news in his or her own tongue. God met everyone exactly where they were, as the divine continues to do.

For reflection: Paul writes that in Christ "there is no longer Jew or Greek . . . no longer slave or free . . . no longer male and female, for all are one in Christ." Compare this to the unity in the presence of diversity in the Pentecost story. How are we to respect differences while also embracing unity?

Trinity Sunday: Celebrating life

Year A: Genesis 1:1–2:4; Year B: John 3:1–17

Trinity Sunday, the first Sunday after Pentecost, is the gateway from Easter Season to Ordinary Time, with a wide variety of readings that either implicitly or explicitly engage with the three Persons of the Trinity, ranging from the first chapter of Genesis where the spirit of God hovers over the face of the waters to Jesus's conversation with Nicodemus where he likens the spirit to the wind. The doctrine of the Trinity has confounded theologians for centuries.

I heard a good summary of the relationship between the members of the Trinity while experiencing noon prayer at a Benedictine abbey during the week after Pentecost a number of years ago. The liturgy closes with this benediction:

In the name of Your Son, our Savior, Jesus Christ,
Who lives and reigns and celebrates life,
With You and the Holy Spirit,
One God, forever and ever, Amen.

It was the notion that the Father, Son, and Holy Spirit "celebrate life" together that caught my attention that day. If they are setting an example, how is life to be celebrated, particularly in the middle of the daily grind when there seems to be little to celebrate?

Toward the end of his collection of essays, Michel de Montaigne reflects on his own life and describes what he believes makes a life worth celebrating:

The most beautiful of lives to my liking are those which conform to the common measure, human and ordinate, without miracles, though, and without rapture.

Montaigne is not suggesting that mountain-top experiences are unimportant; rather, he is reminding us that a beautiful life is not constructed from such experiences. There is a reason why the majority of the Christian liturgical year, although seasoned with the miracle of the Incarnation and the rapture of Easter, is spent in long stretches of getting down to the day-to-day, week-to-week work of being a regular human being trying to live a life in the presence of the divine. As the old saying goes, life is what happens while we are making other plans.

Montaigne believes that the beauty of a life is to be judged by what you are doing between the miracles and the ecstasy. Or, as Jeanne has suggested, it's about the "dash"—the little line that will be carved between the two dates on your tombstone. The majority of every person's days are ordinary, broken up occasionally by highs and lows. We tend to mark the passage of our lives with those highs and lows, but Ordinary Time reminds us that our lives are to be lived and celebrated, not in anticipation or remembrance, but in the present.

The closing paragraph of George Eliot's *Middlemarch* is a clear expression of the sort of life Montaigne considers to be beautiful. Of her heroine, Dorothea Brooke, Eliot writes:

> *Her finely touched spirit had still its fine issues, though they were not widely visible. Her full nature, like that river of which Cyrus broke the strength, spent itself in channels which had no great name on the earth. But the effect of her being on those around her was incalculably diffusive: for the growing good of the world is partly dependent on unhistoric acts; and that things are not so ill with you and me as they might have been, is half owing to the number who lived faithfully a hidden life, and rest in unvisited tombs.*

I find this description of a life beautifully lived in "ordinary time" helpful. I would love to write a bestseller. I would love mine to be the first likeness carved on the Mount Rushmore for Teachers that someone should create sometime. I would love to have thousands of people all over the world waiting with rapt expectation for my next wise and witty blog post. But I would like most to faithfully live a life according to Montaigne's "common measure," bringing what I have to offer into each new day with intelligence, energy, and an occasional infusion of divine humor. There's nothing better than an ordinary day, a day in which one finds a new way to celebrate being alive. Miracles and rapture are fine if you get them, but at the end of the road a "nicely done" would be even better.

For reflection: Jesus consistently likens the "Kingdom of Heaven" to ordinary things. Practice finding the sacred in the ordinary, noting the ways in which those things that we barely notice reflect the presence of the divine.

CHAPTER 7

Ordinary Time—Parables and Miracles

Ordinary Time is by far the longest liturgical season, in some years accounting for more than half of the Sundays in the entire cycle. Depending on the date of Easter, Ordinary Time can include anywhere from twenty-three to twenty-seven Sundays. They are organized according to "Propers"—a brief description of Propers is included in the Notes. The lectionary possibilities for each Sunday of Ordinary Time include many options, particularly with regard to the first reading from the Jewish Scriptures and the Psalms. Although our primary focus in this chapter will remain on the designated gospel readings, important texts from the Jewish Scriptures will occasionally be front and center.

Every year at Easter, Christians celebrate Jesus's resurrection and all we believe that entails. The triumph of life over death. The rupture between the divine and the human healed. It's the culmination of what many have described as the greatest story ever told. It is an event worth celebrating and, for some Christians, is essentially the end of the story (until the apocalypse and last judgment, that is).

But then everyone wakes up the next morning and has the "Now what?" question staring them in the face. Over the centuries, those who shaped the liturgical calendar that frames the attitudes and perspectives of believers through several seasons each year built this question into the weeks after the Easter season. How to sustain the energy when the big "wins" like Christmas and Easter fade into the background? Ordinary Time is an exploration of possible answers to this question.

Proper 4: Do I matter?

Year A: Psalm 139:1–6, 13–18

The appointed Psalm for Proper 4 Year A is Psalm 139, a meditation on perennial questions that plagued the psalmist three thousand years ago and continue to challenge contemporary humans. Am I good enough? More fundamentally, do I matter at all? Just about everyone is familiar with "imposter syndrome," the conviction that although others believe that I am qualified and skilled at what I do, they would think otherwise if they knew the truth. Psalm 139 offers hope in the face of insignificance.

Perhaps there is one place where I do not need to be an impostor or be overwhelmed by my insignificance, a place where I am known better than I know myself and am valued more highly than I could ever manufacture.

> *O LORD, you have searched me and known me.*
> *You know when I sit down and when I rise up;*
> *you discern my thoughts from far away . . .*
> *Where can I go from your spirit? Or where can I flee from your presence?*
> *If I ascend to heaven, you are there; if I make my bed in Sheol, you are there.*
> *If I take the wings of the morning and settle at the farthest limits of the sea,*
> *even there your hand shall lead me, and your right hand shall hold me fast . . .*
> *For it was you who created my being, knit me together in my mother's womb.*

The mere improbability that the creator of the universe cares about insignificant me is overwhelming. If I were inclined to be an atheist, or at least an agnostic, it would probably be because of this very point—the idea that God cares about human beings in any specific sense at all. Most of what we observe and experience screams against it. Our obvious insignificance screams against it. As the seventeenth-century mathematician and philosopher Blaise Pascal put it, "the eternal silence of these infinite spaces frightens me."

My sons grew up on the wonderful books of Dr. Seuss; *Horton Hears a Who* was one of their favorites. Horton the Elephant, while splashing in a pool, hears a small speck of dust talking to him. He comes to realize that the voice is coming from a small person who lives on the dust speck; indeed, the speck is actually a tiny planet, home to a community called Whoville, the home of microscopic creatures called Whos.

The Whos know that they are vulnerable and exposed to possible harm in a dangerous world; the mayor of Whoville asks Horton for protection, which Horton happily agrees to provide. He places the Who-planet on a clover that he proceeds to carry in his trunk as carefully as a waiter carrying a tray of crystal champagne glasses. Each existing thing is the center of its own universe of interests, desires, and concerns—but each existing thing is also just a speck in the universe of possible things. Psalm 139 tells us that

> *You have formed my inward parts;*
> *You have formed me in my mother's womb . . .*
> *My frame was not hidden from you,*
> *When I was made in secret*
> *And skillfully wrought in the lowest parts of the earth.*

Everything is at the same time both insignificant and unique. The challenge is to keep both of these in mind simultaneously.

As Horton's story proceeds, his fellow jungle animals refuse to believe that the Whos exist, believing rather that Horton is crazy. In scenes reminiscent of grade-school playgrounds, various animals ridicule Horton, eventually managing to steal his Who-bearing clover and hide it from him in a large field of clovers. After a long search, Horton rescues the frightened and shaken Whos; at his prompting, they finally prove their existence to the still skeptical jungle animals by making as much collective noise as possible until everyone can hear them. Now convinced of the Whos' existence, all the animals vow to help Horton protect the tiny community.

Each of us is both insignificant and infinitely precious, no matter what current circumstances might indicate. The Whos, upon discovering just how vulnerable and fragile their world is, are discovered by someone greater than themselves, someone willing to put himself on the line again and again to preserve their special existence. It's a wonderful retelling of a story that generations have embraced. "A person's a person no matter how small," after all.

For reflection: Central to both Jewish and Christian faith is the tension between God's transcendence (wholly other) and God's immanence (intimately present). How does this tension show up in your faith journey?

Proper 5: Follow me

Year A: Matthew 9:9–13

The Proper 5 Year A gospel from Matthew is brief and to the point. Jesus walks past the booth in which Matthew is collecting taxes from his fellow Jewish citizens, says "Follow me," and Matthew does. End of story. But a bit of context helps to fill out the story in interesting ways.

As a tax collector, Matthew was a pariah to his fellow Jews. He was a Roman employee whose job was to extract Roman taxes from his fellow Jewish citizens. The booth he was in was undoubtedly protected both by prison-type bars and a Roman soldier. The backstory of how and why an itinerant rabbi could simply say "Follow me" and cause a privileged, wealthy person to drop everything and follow is not provided.

One of the reasons Jeanne and I enjoy *The Chosen* is that the possible backstories of each of the disciples are fully developed, turning each of them into real human beings rather than figures in statues or stained-glass windows. Every person who finds themselves seeking to follow Jesus, from two thousand years ago to the present, has their own "Follow me" story. Here is one of my favorites.

Blaise Pascal was one of the great mathematicians of the Scientific Revolution who, on November 23, 1654, had a powerful encounter with something greater than himself that changed his life. Pascal's encounter has come to be known as his "Night of Fire." He wrote a description of his experience down on a piece of parchment and sewed it into his coat, where it was found after his death eight years later.

Pascal became a committed apologist for the Christian faith; because he died at the early age of thirty-eight, he never was able to finish his reflections on how he—a person of remarkable intelligence—wove his reason and his new-found faith together. His scattered writings were collected into a volume we know as the *Pensées* after his death.

Perhaps the best-known sentence from the *Pensées* is Pascal's observation that "the heart has reasons that reason does not know." Pascal frequently expands on this, writing, for instance,

> We know the truth, not only through reason, but also through the heart. It is through the latter that we know first principles, and reason, which has no part in it, tries

> *in vain to challenge them. Reason must use this knowledge from the heart and instinct, and base all its arguments on it.*

People of faith are often criticized because they arguably base their faith on principles or experiences for which they can provide no rational supporting evidence. The person of faith often responds defensively by trying to provide such supporting evidence, knowing all along that the critic is right. The core of faith cannot be expressed, nor can it be supported, in an exclusively rational manner.

Pascal's insight is that the problem is not with the person of faith's irrationality. Rather, the problem is the critic's refusal to accept that there are more kinds of evidence than rational and more sources of belief than reason. The source of faith conviction is what Pascal calls the heart, a source of belief and evidence every bit as legitimate as reason and logic. Pascal writes,

> *Principles are felt, propositions are proved; all with certainty, though in different ways. And it is as useless and absurd for reason to demand from the heart proofs of its first principles before accepting them, as it would be for the heart to demand from reason an intuition of all demonstrated propositions before receiving them.*

The best "proof" of faith is a changed life. Only the person who inhabits that life can tell the story of how she or he came to embrace principles at the center of their life that are felt rather than proved. The critic owes such a person a hearing; this requires admitting, at least for the sake of argument, that, as Hamlet tells Horatio, "there are more things in heaven and earth than are dreamed of in your philosophy."

The gospel texts of Ordinary Time are full of stories in which someone's life is turned upside-down and changed forever just because they happened to encounter Jesus. When asked to explain what happened, such people seldom have a logical explanation. Instead, they are like the formerly blind man in John's gospel who, upon being told that the man who healed him is a sinner, replies, "Whether he is a sinner, I do not know; one thing I know, that though I was blind, now I see." Sometimes the only convincing proof is a story.

*For reflection: **What is the best way to account for one's faith: by providing an argument or telling a story?***

Proper 6: The fruit of the spirit

Year C: Galatians 5:13–25

The Proper 6 Year C New Testament reading is from Paul's letter to the Galatians, where Paul lists the "fruit of the spirit" after he writes that "if you are led by the spirit, you are not subject to the law." The "fruit of the spirit" passage was one that I memorized in Sunday School as a youth, but it was not until struggling with a particularly stubborn berry bush in my backyard that I gained some insight into the dynamics of bearing fruit.

A number of years ago, Jeanne returned from a weekend with a friend in Vermont with a little plant in a box—a Vermont blackberry bush. It has been trying to take over our backyard ever since. After surviving its first winter, our new blackberry bush awakened to spring by busting out all over with new leaves, shoots that grew so quickly that I could almost hear them doing it, and random offspring (officially called "suckers") sticking their little unwanted green heads up as far as ten feet away from the mother bush. The suckers had neither regard for my plans and lawn design nor respect for the personal space of their neighbors.

It's been a few years now. Every spring I pull up random shoots from the blackberry bush in the lawn but have allowed two or three new shoots to stay in the flower beds—shoots that have grown as large as the original.

It doesn't help that for some reason, this plant is Jeanne's favorite of the dozens of items in our back and front yards. If it were up to her, our backyard would contain nothing but our blackberry bush and its offspring. While I am annoyed with its aggressiveness and the work I have to put in to keep it under control, she sees nothing but its beauty and productivity—that this plant, as unruly as it is, usually produces wonderful fruit (unless feathered or four-legged things get it first). I marvel annually at the methodical, predictable, and completely miraculous way in which plants emerge from the ground, grow, produce buds, then flower, all the time "neither toiling nor spinning," as Jesus pointed out.

After praising the wonders of blackberry making, Jeanne made a connection to "the fruit of the Spirit" as described in Paul's letter to the Galatians. "I just realized something for the first time," she said. "The fruit of the Spirit is not something the Spirit brings us; the fruit of the Spirit develops in you as the natural process of a person living in tune with the Spirit inside them."

This is a great insight, since many of us who have heard about the fruit of the spirit our whole lives tend to think of it as something describing what the Spirit produces for us. Rather, the fruit of the Spirit—love, joy, patience, kindness, generosity, gentleness, faithfulness, and self-control—are the natural fruits produced by those who live their lives energized by the Spirit within.

The natural activity of our blackberry bush, its ebb and flow, its dormant as well as active seasons, and its frequent need for tending and pruning, are all directly comparable to the life of the Spirit. There are seasons when nothing happens, as well as seasons when exuberance causes us to extend our resources in ways that need eventually to be cut back. Sending out "spiritual suckers" into territory for which we are not prepared or equipped, only to have our well-intentioned forays foiled by what knows better, is an experience anyone who seeks to live faith rather than just think about it is familiar with.

So often we get impatient with ourselves because our natural American results-oriented energy has little or no place in the plant-like processes of the Spirit. We differ from plants because we can choose to cooperate with or resist the Spirit within us—a plant just does what it is fully equipped to do without worrying from day to day if it is doing it right.

Patience and confidence go hand in hand as we proceed from the first signs of fruit to full maturity, then cycle back to do it all over again. As Paul writes elsewhere, "[T]he one who began a good work among you will bring it to completion." I'm glad that the cosmic gardener has more patience with me than I have with our blackberry bush.

For reflection: All gardeners know that vigorous pruning of flowering and fruit bearing bushes and trees is necessary to both the health and growth of the plant. Jesus often likens this process to the life of faith—in what ways have you found that the pain and suffering of pruning have led to a healthier faith journey?

Proper 7: Jesus and family values

Year A: Matthew 10:35–39

The gospel readings during Ordinary Time regularly include difficult teachings from Jesus. For instance, in the Proper 7 Year A reading from Matthew, Jesus says that

> *I have come to set a man against his father, and a daughter against her mother, and a daughter-in-law against her mother-in-law; and one's foes will be members of one's own household. Whoever loves father or mother more than me is not worthy of me; and whoever loves son or daughter more than me is not worthy of me.*

In the Year C reading from Luke's gospel the following Sunday, Jesus tells a would-be follower whose father has just died that he should "let the dead bury their own dead" rather than delaying following Jesus in order to attend to his father's funeral. It is enough to make one wonder what Jesus thought about "family values."

In the estimation of many, "family values" are *conservative* values, focusing on respect for authority, hard work, independence, patriotism, faith, and so on, but during every political cycle liberal and progressive voices are heard crying out that *true* family values are about concern for others, lifting the downtrodden, and speaking truth to power. And the never-ending war over who truly defines and owns family values rages on. But what do family values prescribe concerning my relationship with my actual family? Because it is pretty clear from the Gospels that Jesus didn't necessarily value family relationships as highly as we might expect or demand.

The "What would Jesus do?" ("WWJD?") concept has been popular for some time, intended to remind the follower of Jesus that moral behavior for a person of Christian faith is a matter of imitating Jesus as presented in the Gospels. One can find WWJD? coffee cups, posters, key chains, bumper stickers, T-shirts, wrist bands—the idea has been viral for a long time. But do we really want to do what Jesus did?

For example, should a person say to his or her mother, "Woman, what concern is that to you?" when she asks for a favor? Should we encourage twelve-year-olds to speak to their parents rudely and dismissively as Jesus did to Mary and Joseph during the Temple episode? Should we tell a person mourning the recent death of his or her father to "Let the dead bury their dead"? If one is concerned about family values, WWJD? at times might be a better guide for what one should *not* do.

Attempts to ground one's own moral code, regardless of its content, in the example of Jesus from the gospel stories often are little more than thinly veiled attempts to create Jesus in one's own image. For every gospel text congruent with our traditional understanding of family values (and there are many such texts), there is a text in which Jesus promises that following him and seeking God is guaranteed to turn one's world upside-down and to violate almost every traditional moral expectation and norm.

Everyone is aware of families torn apart and destroyed when one of the family members sets out on a mission to "accomplish God's work." The stories of Jesus give ample justification for ignoring one's family obligations and connections if they conflict with the perceived will of God for one's life. The legendary football coach Vince Lombardi used to tell his Green Bay Packers players that their priorities were to be "God, Family, and the Green Bay Packers"—although his players report that frequently he clearly changed the order. Is God a cosmic Vince Lombardi insisting upon being at the pinnacle of a rigid hierarchy, to the detriment of anything else, no matter how important, that might conflict?

Maybe. But what if Jesus's consistently violating our values and expectations is a call to consider something more radical than our limited imaginations can accommodate? If rather than residing at "the top of the heap," God is everything and everything is in God, then the lay of the land is no longer a landscape of "either/or." The answer to the question "which is more important, God or family?" is "yes." Jesus's provocative statements concerning the family are intended to demonstrate that when we include God as just another object of important things that need to be placed in proper order, we are misconstruing God entirely.

If everything is in God, then God is not ultimately in conflict with anything. If God and family appear to be in conflict, then faith tells me that somewhere, at some level, God and family are in unity regardless of appearances. If I have to regularly choose between paying attention to God and to my job, then my faith-energized assignment is to learn how to find God *in* my job (since my job is in God, as is everything else). Attempts to fit the life of faith into familiar categories, even if we are willing to significantly adjust those categories, miss the boat. The energy of the Christian life is captured well by the Apostle Paul: *And I will show you a more excellent way.*

> *For reflection: I learned a song in Sunday School that said, "Jesus, and Others, and You—what a wonderful way to spell JOY." Consider this hierarchy in light of Jesus's "difficult teachings." Does the song have it right, or is there more to consider?*

Proper 8: The fertility of silence

Year C: I Kings 19:1–21

The Proper 8 Year C reading from the Jewish Scriptures contains the conclusion of a story that has much to teach about both physical and spiritual dynamics, a story that spans the entire nineteenth chapter of 1 Kings. We find the prophet Elijah exhausted, fearful for his life, and hiding from Queen Jezebel. Elijah has just scored a major victory over the forces of idolatry and for Yahweh by destroying the prophets of Baal on top of Mount Carmel. And Queen Jezebel wants him dead.

One day into his flight, Elijah gives up. "Yesterday I was on my way to the propheting gold medal," he complains, "but today it isn't working." He collapses into a fetal position under a broom tree and has a classic drama queen moment: "It is enough; now, O LORD, take away my life, for I am no better than my ancestors." The divine response is interesting. An angel shows up, cooks Elijah some food, then wakes him, saying, "Get up and eat." Elijah wants to die and the angel makes him a meal. Sometimes it's as simple as that—eat properly, rest, get some exercise, take your medication, and get over yourself. Elijah may not be better than his ancestors, but he is still loved by God.

With his physical needs taken care of, Elijah continues to flee from Jezebel, eventually ending up in a cave, where God asks him a very odd question. "What are you doing here, Elijah?" Elijah's response, paraphrased, shows his frustration and anger at everything, including God. "I've been the only one in the kingdom seeking to do your will, I've torn down their altars, I've killed the priests of Baal just as you told me to, *and she's trying to kill me!*" Is that any way to treat your favorite prophet?

In response, God says, "Come over here on top of this hill—I want to show you something." In succession, Elijah experiences a rock-shattering wind, an earthquake, and a fire—perhaps similar to the fire that brought the victory on Mount Carmel a few days earlier. But "the Lord was not in the wind," or the earthquake, or the fire. All of these are followed by "a still small voice," or as another translation puts it, "sheer silence." And in the midst of that silence, Elijah knows what he is to do.

There is a Lenten prayer in the Benedictine cycle of daily petitions that asks God to make us responsive to "the fertility of silence." Silence is divinely fertile because it shatters our expectation that God is transactional, that if we ask for X properly, we'll get it. The transactional God is a projection of our human need to find at least a small part of reality that we can control. This is understandable, since the obvious truth that we are small fish in a large ocean of reality is never far below the level of consciousness. Anne Lamott quotes a friend who says that "you can safely assume you've created God in your own image when it turns out that God hates all the same people you do."

There is a reason why the first commandment is a prohibition against graven images—human beings are incurable idolaters. The ancient Israelites found Baal attractive because they thought they had him figured out and could control him. Elijah in the cave was upset because he thought he had God on a leash and found out otherwise. God is not transactional—God is indwelling.

God is with me wherever I go, but never in ways reducible to formulas. As Jacob said after encountering the divine in a dream, "surely the Lord is in this place and I did not know it."

A third grader once told Kathleen Norris that "silence reminds me to take my soul with me wherever I go." This is good to remember when my life gets overwhelmed by noise and distractions, as is the following from Psalm 131:

> *I have calmed and quieted my soul, like a weaned child with its mother. My soul is like the weaned child that is with me.*

When I remember that God is in the space of silence and peace within, I realize that the divine's response to my need is something entirely unexpected but absolutely God-like.

For reflection: It is difficult in our noisy and demanding world to create spaces of silence. Yet we are told regularly in Scripture that it is in silence where we are most likely to encounter the divine. Where are the places in your life where it might be possible to create a silence in which to wait for and hear God?

Proper 9: Blessed with a burden

Year A: Matthew 11:25–30

On one level, Ordinary Time can seem like a collection of Jesus's "greatest hits"—his most famous sayings, stories, and miracles week after week. Proper 9 is no exception. The Year A gospel reading from Matthew concludes with Jesus's well-known pronouncement that, despite all appearances, "my yoke is easy, and my burden is light."

"The Calling of Saint Matthew," a painting by Renaissance master Caravaggio, is a brilliant example of chiaroscuro. Chiaroscuro is a painting technique that uses strong contrasts between light and dark, illumination and shadow, bold contrasts that affect the whole composition. In Caravaggio's masterpiece, the light shining from a window outside the top right of the canvas illuminates just enough of Jesus's modest halo to make clear who he is, as well as the expressions on the faces of everyone at the table. But this light also makes the shadows even darker and more pronounced. Light does not dispel the darkness; rather, it changes everything. This light has transformed the life of the man on whom it is directed—for better and for worse.

Once, several years ago, the marquee sign outside of church announced the key passage for that Sunday: "My yoke is easy and my burden is light." Jeanne told me after church that upon seeing the sign, she had one of those "a-ha!" moments that ran counter to the usual interpretation of the famous line. She (and probably everyone else aware of the passage and its context) always assumed that Jesus meant that the burden of following him is not heavy—it's light. And that's what the Greek text implies as well.

But thanks to the wonders of the English language, this passage can mean something entirely different and much more interesting. What if Jesus means that it is our burden—our duty—to illuminate the darkness, to bring light into a world that badly needs it? What if we read "light" in "my burden is light" as a noun rather than as an adjective? There are all sorts of light-related references attributed to Jesus, including that we are "the light of the world." And yet Caravaggio and others show us through their skillful use of chiaroscuro that being a light-bearer comes with a built-in price—illuminating the darkness also involves revealing the shadows, both in oneself and in others. Sometimes commitment and faithfulness come with a cost.

Jeanne went on to say that her new reading of "My burden is light" reminded her of an important scene from one of our favorite movies. *Freedom Writers* is the story of Erin Gruwell, played in the movie by Hilary Swank. Erin is a young, idealistic teacher in South Los Angeles in the 1990s who finds her enthusiasm and creativity stretched to the breaking point by students divided into gangs along racial lines and an administration that refuses to let Gruwell give the students books to read because the books might be stolen or damaged. Her unorthodox teaching methods incrementally have a positive impact on her students, but there is a price to be paid.

Toward the end of the movie, Erin is having dinner with her father and breaks into tears. Her husband has left her due to her 24/7 dedication to her job and a lack of time for him and their marriage. She sits, weeping, asking her father, "Has any of this been worth it? Does it even matter? Have I made any difference?" Her father, who up to this point has been less than supportive of Erin's commitment, looks at her and says, "You have been blessed with a burden, my daughter. I envy and admire that."

Jesus told his followers, "You are the light of the world." Persons of faith are also blessed with a burden—a burden of light. This is not a burden of things to do, actions to perform, or positions to take, any more than light considers illumination to be its job. Many centuries ago, Aristotle resonated with this insight when he argued that the moral life is far less about what a person *does* than it is about that person's character, about who that person *is*. Just as light changes everything it comes into contact with just by being what it is, so too the person of character reveals herself and introduces light into the darkness simply by being, by showing up.

And this is the call to persons of faith. Be there; show up; remember that we have the divine within us. The light may be dim, flickering, all but invisible, but it is the way in which the divine invades the darkness. It doesn't simply remove darkness; indeed, it reveals new shadows and dark places that could not be seen before the light arrived. But our burden, shadows and all, is to be what we have chosen to be—divine light bearers.

For reflection: What are the burdens that you have been blessed with? How does being a person of faith simultaneously restrict and bless you?

Proper 10: The Good Samaritan

Year C: Luke 10:25–37

The Proper 10 Year C gospel from Luke is one of Jesus's most beloved parables. Is there any parable more familiar than the story of the Good Samaritan? And is there any parable whose message is more difficult to live out? Jesus uses the story to illustrate mercy, the second virtue in the prophet Micah's directive to "do justice, love kindness/mercy, and walk humbly with your God." Jesus agrees with the man who concludes that the true neighbor in the story was "the one who showed mercy." But consider the Good Samaritan story with the last of Micah's virtues in view: humility.

On its face, humility is not a popular virtue; indeed, self-effacement, being a doormat, deference to others—all popular synonyms for humility—seem more like vices than a virtue. Humility is not included in Aristotle's famous list of virtues, and philosophers for millennia have struggled with humility, often ignoring it or altogether denying that it is a virtue. It certainly doesn't fit comfortably with the dominant American notions of independence, individuality, competition, and aggressive achievement. And yet one can scarcely read a page of the Psalms or the New Testament without encountering calls for humility. So, what exactly is being called for?

In the Good Samaritan story, the priest, the Levite, and the Samaritan all see the man beaten, robbed, and left for dead in the ditch. And yet their manner of seeing is very different. The story says that in the case of both the priest and the Levite, "when he saw him, he passed by on the other side." The most common scholarly explanation for their behavior is that both the priest and the Levite assumed that the man was dead and did not want to violate the many prohibitions in the Torah against those who handled holy things for a living touching anything dead. In other words, the priest and the Levite saw the injured man through the lenses of their societal roles and commitments. They saw the injured man with the eyes of the self.

"But a Samaritan while traveling came near him; and when he saw him, he was moved with pity." Travelling on the road between Jerusalem and Jericho, the Samaritan was in enemy territory—Samaritans and Jews had nothing to do with each other. They were "Others" to each other. The man in the ditch was almost certainly the sort of person that the Samaritan had been taught to hate. The Samaritan is on a journey, undoubtedly in a hurry, with miles to go before he sleeps—why does he stop? What does he see that the priest and the Levite did not see?

As simple as it sounds, the Samaritan stopped because he saw the injured man unfiltered. Simone Weil calls this ability to see unfiltered "attention," and suggests that it is at the heart of true human connection. Another word for this ability to see unfiltered, to attentively look at what is in front of me unencumbered by my usual filters and agendas, is *humility*. And it is at the heart of true faith.

This is why defining ourselves morally in terms of positions taken on hot-button issues is far more attractive than actually attempting to live a life guided by what the texts and principles of one's faith demand. Human beings are not naturally wired in this way. Iris Murdoch writes that

> [w]e live in a dream, we're wrapped up in a dark veil, we think we're omnipotent magicians, we don't believe anything exists except ourselves. Our attachments tend to be selfish and strong, and the transformation of our lives from selfishness to unselfishness is sometimes hard even to conceive of.

This is what makes the Good Samaritan miraculous—he is able to truly see what is in front of him and respond directly without a moment's concern for anything other than what this man needs.

Iris Murdoch defines love as "the extremely difficult realization that something other than oneself is real." Love and humility, in other words, go hand in hand. Love and humility energize the apprehension of something else, something particular as existing outside us. In our daily lives, we are *continually* confronting something other than ourselves. We all not only can but *must* deal with the resistant otherness of other people, other things, history, the natural world, and this involves a perpetual effort. But at the heart of the Christian faith, illustrated by the parable of the Good Samaritan, is the promise that the possibility of transformative love and humility is in each of us, ready to be introduced into the world if we will only look away from ourselves toward what is directly in front of us.

For reflection: The Good Samaritan story is Jesus's response to the question, "Who is my neighbor?" Why do you think Jesus chose a hated outsider to embody the answer to this question?

Proper 11: Sowing and reaping

Year A: Matthew 13:1–9 (Proper 10); 13:24–30 (Proper 11)

The Proper 11 Year A gospel reading from Matthew 13 is a companion to the Proper 10 Year A parable from earlier in the chapter that is high on the "Jesus's most famous parables" list. Jesus's stories are frequently rooted in the rhythms and processes of the natural world, implying that we might learn a great deal about the Creator by close observation of the world around us. The parable of the weeds among the wheat and the parable of the sower immerse the reader in the cycle of seed to harvest, telling us not only something about the divine economy but also reminding us that whatever God's strategies are, they do not include efficiency, maximum yield, or the bottom line.

The parable of the sower is so familiar that it is easy to miss some of the most striking details. The sower is apparently just throwing seeds out there roughly in the direction of where fertile ground might be, but his activity is remarkably inefficient, based on the yield Jesus goes on to describe. But if, as Jesus's interpretation later in the chapter suggests, the seed is the word of God, then this is just the typical divine strategy that we keep bumping into—"Let's just throw a bunch of stuff out there indiscriminately and see what happens!"

God is no respecter of persons, statistics, focus groups, yield projections, bounce rates, polls, or any other thing humans might devise as the best predictor of effectiveness and efficiency. Consider, for instance, the extraordinary open-endedness and seeming wastefulness of the way God chose to crank out endless varieties of living things—natural selection—to realize that Isaiah wasn't kidding when he reports God as saying that "my thoughts are not your thoughts, neither are your ways my ways."

Years ago, I got to know a number of the monks and priests who served as liaisons between their onsite abbey and the ecumenical institute where I was in residence. One of the monks had recently retired from several decades of teaching physics at the university as well as the prep school nearby. During one lunch conversation, he noted that "Darwin taught us more about God than all of the theologians put together." When I asked him to expand on his claim, he proposed a thought experiment: Forget for a minute everything you've ever been told about what God is like and start over. Suppose that Darwin's theory of evolution by natural selection is largely correct. On the basis of what that theory tells us about the world, what might we speculate concerning the preferences, interests, and personality traits of God?

Most immediately, the evolutionary process indicates that God prefers change over stability, novelty over the expected and familiar, process over completion, and imperfection over perfection. Annie Dillard writes that

> *[n]ot only did the creator create everything, but he is apt to create* anything. *He'll stop at nothing. There is no one standing over evolution with a blue pencil to say: "Now, that one, there, is absolutely ridiculous, and I won't have it."*

Within the parameters of physical laws, the Creator apparently is committed to freedom and creativity above all else—not just in human beings, but in everything. Within very broad parameters, life never stops recreating itself in new forms. As the Jesuit paleontologist Teilhard de Chardin observed, "Properly speaking, God does not make: He makes things that make themselves."

Much of this flies in the face of traditional conceptions of God that do not include open-endedness, change, or provisionality. The God generated by the thought experiment is, however, what one of my students once described as "a more interesting God," an observation expressed by Anglican priest and theoretical physicist John Polkinghorne:

> *God is not the puppet master of the universe, pulling every string. God has taken, if you like, a risk. Creation is more like an improvisation than the performance of a fixed score that God wrote in eternity.*

An improvisational creation makes room for radical freedom and creativity, not just in human beings but at the very basic, foundational level of creation itself. Why would God choose to create using such a non-economical, inefficient, and open-ended process? Because God values freedom and beauty above all else.

For reflection: In the final paragraph of **The Origin of Species,** *Darwin says the following about the theory of evolution by natural selection: "There is grandeur in this view of life . . . whilst this planet has gone cycling on according to the fixed law of gravity, from so simple a beginning endless forms* *most beautiful and most wonderful have been, and are being, evolved." Do you agree?*

Proper 12: The Kingdom of Heaven is like . . .

Year A: Matthew 13:31–33, 44–52

In the Proper 12 Year A reading from Matthew 13, Jesus likens the Kingdom of heaven to all sorts of things. "The Kingdom of Heaven is like . . ." a mustard seed, yeast, a pearl, a net thrown into the sea, and so on. The official name for this series of "likes" in Matthew is "The Similitudes," familiar illustrations of how, over time, unremarkable things (and persons) can have remarkable and unexpected effects on their surroundings. But as is always the case, there's more to see just a bit below the surface.

Jesus notes that the mustard seed "is the smallest of all the seeds, but when it has grown it is the greatest of shrubs and becomes a tree, so that the birds of the air come and make nests in its branches." One year, the rector of my church had a single mustard seed taped to the front of each bulletin when the Similitudes were the gospel reading just so each parishioner could see how tiny the seed actually is. Modern readers generally only know about mustard as a condiment, but Jesus's contemporaries would have been jerked up short by Jesus's parable because the mustard plant is a *weed*. It's not as if Jesus is saying that "the Kingdom of Heaven is like a tiny seed that, over time, grows into something useful." He's saying that "the kingdom of Heaven is like a weed that no farmer wants in their field."

The mustard plant is native to the Middle East and Asia and was introduced to North America sometime in the twentieth century (probably freeloading along with some plant from across the ocean that people here actually wanted). Various websites note that wild mustard overwhelms wildflowers, useful grains, and other desirable plants by monopolizing moisture and producing seeds more quickly than its competitors, as well as by growing more quickly than surrounding plants, robbing them of needed sunshine and nutrients. In other words, when Jesus compares the Kingdom of Heaven to a mustard seed, he's saying that the Kingdom of Heaven is sort of like Audrey II, the carnivorous plant in *The Little Shop of Horrors*.

In *The Parables of the Kingdom*, theologian C. H. Dodd writes that,

> [a]t its simplest, a parable is a metaphor or simile, drawn from nature or the common life, arresting the hearer by its vividness or strangeness, and leaving the mind in sufficient doubt about its precise application to tease it into active thought.

Supposing that, as Jesus often said, the Kingdom of Heaven is about now and not about some future world, as well as an analogy for living out the life of following Jesus, what might we learn from Jesus comparing the Kingdom of Heaven to a fast-growing and aggressive weed? First, *the Kingdom of Heaven is unpredictable.* To use another familiar simile, following Jesus is like Forrest Gump's box of chocolates. You never know what you're going to get. The life of faith is almost never what one expects it to be—just as Jesus warned. It is so unpredictable and unrewarding measured by normal expectations that Teresa of Avila reportedly told God in a prayer that "if this is how you treat your friends, it is no wonder you have so few."

Second, *the Kingdom of Heaven cannot be harnessed or domesticated.* It is often surprising and even amusing to experience just how disrespectful the divine appears to be of our various attempts to domesticate and harness our interactions with what is greater than us. Liturgy? Doctrine? Dogma? As soon as you think you've got it figured out, be looking for ways in which real engagement with faith and the divine does an end run on our systems and expectations.

Finally, *the Kingdom of Heaven is risky, even dangerous.* I discover every semester that the majority of my students, many of whom are products of twelve years of Catholic parochial education, believe that "comfort" is the primary reason to be a person of faith. In response, I often draw their attention to what Jesus actually said to those who wanted to follow him in the Gospels. Be prepared to give everything up, including your life, if you are a follower of Jesus. Everything is on the table and up for grabs—no one gets out of here unchanged. Those who mistakenly thought that the mustard plant was innocuous and harmless soon found out otherwise. Those who think that the life of faith will be an attractive, sometimes entertaining hobby find themselves denying everything and taking up their cross.

For reflection: Which of the many "Similitudes" do you find most helpful and/or thought-provoking in your own faith journey? Why?

Proper 13: Feeding the five thousand

Year A: Matthew 14:13–21; Year B: John 6:1–14

The Proper 13 Year A and B gospel is one of Jesus's most famous miracles: the feeding of the five thousand. This miracle is reported in all four of the canonical Gospels, which, for once, pretty much agree on the details. As is the case with all miracles, we are presented with a straightforward story of something happening that simply could not have happened. Simone Weil once wrote that "the stories of miracles complicate everything." She's right. Ever since my youth I have asked, "What are we supposed to do with such stories, especially since we don't see people raised from the dead or storms dispersed by a voice command today? Did these things really happen? If so, why don't they happen now?"

I once heard a Benedictine priest give a homily on the feeding of the five thousand. He struggled mightily with the very notion that so many people could be fed with five loaves and two fishes from a kid's picnic basket. After setting things up eloquently and paying proper attention to Jesus's compassion for the crowd of hungry people, he hit a wall with the miracle itself. "We modern persons have a difficult time with the stories of Jesus's miracles," he said, "since what they describe violates the laws of nature." Accordingly, the homilist did what most of us do when faced with such an apparent violation—he provided alternative interpretations of the story in which such a violation did *not* occur.

It is possible, for instance, unless Jesus was dealing with a crowd of fools that day, that the little boy was not the only person among the thousands in attendance smart enough to have brought along something to eat. The "miracle" is not that a tiny amount of food was increased to feed thousands, but rather that the boy's innocent generosity sparked similar generosity in others. Those who had intended to hoard their carefully packed lunches for themselves were suddenly motivated, either through inspiration or shame, to share with others around them.

And then perhaps a further "miracle" occurred, in that many realized that they didn't really need all the food they had brought—five loaves and two fishes are more than one person can eat, right? So as a spirit of generosity spreads through the crowd, gluttony takes a big hit. If each person eats only what they need and shares the remainder, everyone has enough. An impromptu community is built on the spot, everyone learns to share with others as well as to stop eating too much, and no laws of nature are violated.

Why was the homilist, and why are we, always inclined to explain a miracle away, to bring it within the confines of what we believe we know and can explain? This is partly a failure of humility, an insistence that we are the center of the universe and that, as Protagoras infamously claimed, we humans are "the measure of all things." But we aren't. We are subject to the laws of nature, but they are neither defined by nor limited to our experience and understanding.

Still, our dogged attempts to explain (or explain away) everything smells more like fear than lack of humility. What better way to carve a home out of a reality far beyond our control than to define it in terms of what we *can* control? And while humility is the antidote for hubris, the cure for fear is wonder. Fear turns us inward; wonder turns us outward, toward the infinitely fascinating reality in which we find ourselves. And ultimately, wonder turns us toward God, who crosses the vast distance between divine and human by infusing everything, including us, with transcendence. This is the miracle of incarnation, that God inhabits everything, that we are living sacraments, testimonies to divine love.

Thomas Jefferson once published an edition of the Gospels with all the miracles taken out, resulting in a very brief book. A daily existence from which miracles have been removed is similarly impoverished. A good friend of mine who passed away a few years ago defined a miracle as "something that everyone says will never, ever, ever happen and it happens anyways." And that covers just about everything, from individual acts of generosity, through impromptu human solidarity, to feeding thousands with a kid's lunch. Poet Gerard Manley Hopkins wrote, "The earth is charged with the grandeur of God." We need only learn to see it with the eyes of wonder and humility.

For reflection: Marilynne Robinson writes, "Wherever you turn your eyes the world can shine like transfiguration. You don't have to bring a thing to it except a little willingness to see." If we are surrounded by miracles, how can we practice seeing them?

Proper 14: Walking on water

Year A: Matthew 14:22–33

The Proper 14 Year A gospel is Matthew's account of Jesus walking on water, a miracle included in all of the canonical Gospels except Luke. Of the three Synoptic Gospels, Mark is the earliest (around 65–70 CE), with Matthew and Luke coming along fifteen years or so later. It is clear from the texts that both Matthew and Luke used Mark as the spine of their own Gospels, adding in various sayings of Jesus that scholars attribute to another early (undiscovered) source called "Q" (for "Quelle," the German word for "source") as well as other additional material. Mark's and Matthew's treatments of Jesus walking on water provide a good illustration.

Mark's account is, as usual, straightforward, unvarnished, and open-ended in its implications:

> *When evening came, the boat was out on the sea, and he was alone on the land. When he saw that they were straining at the oars against an adverse wind, he came towards them early in the morning, walking on the sea. But when they saw him walking on the sea, they thought it was a ghost and cried out; for they saw him and were terrified. But immediately he spoke to them and said, "Take heart, it is I; do not be afraid." Then he got into the boat with them and the wind ceased. And they were utterly astounded, for they did not understand about the loaves, but their hearts were hardened.*

As is often the case in Mark's gospel, the disciples are unsure of what they are dealing with. "Their hearts were hardened" is not so much a description of disbelief as of total disorientation and confusion.

Matthew's account of the same event is so similar to Mark's account at the beginning that I would accuse Matthew of plagiarism if he was one of my students.

> *When evening came, he was there alone, but by this time the boat, battered by the waves, was far from the land, for the wind was against them. And early in the morning he came walking toward them on the sea. But when the disciples saw him walking on the sea, they were terrified, saying, "It is a ghost!" And they cried out in fear. But immediately Jesus spoke to them and said, "Take heart, it is I; do not be afraid."*

Then Matthew adds a new twist that is central to most retellings of the miracle.

> *Peter answered him, "Lord, if it is you, command me to come to you on the water." He said, "come." So Peter got out of the boat, started walking on the water, and came toward Jesus. But when he noticed the strong wind, he became frightened, and beginning to sink, he cried out, "Lord, save me!" Immediately Jesus stretched out his hand and caught him, and said to him, "O you of little faith, why did you doubt?" After they got into the boat, the wind died down. Those who were in the boat did him homage, saying, "Truly, you are the Son of God."*

So let's get this straight. Peter got out of the boat and walked on the water, and Mark didn't include it in his gospel? That seems like a kind of big thing to leave out or forget. But even more important is Matthew's account of how the disciples reacted to all of this. Mark's disciples are afraid, astounded, clueless, and hard of heart. Matthew's disciples are afraid at first, but after everything is over, they get it. They recognize who Jesus is and worship him.

It is worth remembering that, despite the protestations of many Christians, the Bible was not written for us. The Bible is a library of various books written over many centuries, books originally intended for very specific audiences in very specific social and historical circumstances. One way of engaging with the differences between Mark's and Matthew's versions of Jesus walking on the water is to imagine what sorts of people or communities each version reflects.

Mark's gospel frequently describes the uncertainty and disorientation of those who engaged with and followed Jesus. Sometimes Jesus himself seems unsure about who he is and what his mission is supposed to accomplish. The disciples in Mark's account, just as undoubtedly many early followers of Jesus in the next generation after he was gone, knew that there was something unusual and special going on, but were not yet fully prepared to put a name to it.

By the time Matthew's gospel is written fifteen or more years after Mark's, there is clearly more confidence about who Jesus was that is missing in earlier accounts. Matthew's disciples are more definitive about Jesus's identity than Mark's because collective decisions about Jesus's identity have become more and more definitive and central in early Jesus communities in the intervening years.

Faith evolves and grows over time, accounting for increased experiences and maturity. If your faith is the same now as it was when you first became a person of faith, you have chosen to remain perpetually in the nursery or kindergarten of faith. In the end, the details of what happened during the storm on that lake almost two thousand years ago don't matter nearly as much as what people of faith do with the stories over the succeeding generations. That is what makes such stories continually and eternally new.

For reflection: At the beginning of "The Moth Radio Hour," the host says, "the following stories are true as remembered and experienced by the storyteller." How reliable is memory? What relevance does this have to the truth of the Gospels?

Proper 15: Jesus has a bad day

Year A: Matthew 15:10–28

In the Proper 15 Year A gospel reading from Matthew, Jesus and his entourage travel north from his usual home base around the Sea of Galilee to "the district of Tyre and Sidon" (a dozen miles or so north of the border of Israel into Lebanon on a modern map) after yet another round of dealing with Pharisee complaints. Jesus is both emotionally and physically exhausted, and it shows.

As the group presses forward, a woman elbows her way to within shouting distance of Jesus. Her accent and clothing show that she is a non-Jewish Canaanite (there are many of them in that region), but that doesn't stop her from doing whatever she can to attract Jesus's attention. Her daughter is ill, and she knows by reputation that this itinerant rabbi is also a healer. "Have mercy on me, Lord, Son of David; my daughter is tormented by a demon!" she screams at the top of her lungs. And she keeps screaming—her daughter's health and well-being matter more than the fact that as a woman and as a foreigner, she has no reason to think that anyone, let alone Jesus, will take notice of her.

At first, Jesus simply ignores her. He's too busy, too tired, too annoyed by the crowds, too *something* to be bothered with this woman. But she continues screaming for his help, so much so that it gets embarrassing. "Send her away," a disciple or two mutters to him. "She keeps shouting after us." Finally, Jesus has had enough. Turning to the annoying foreigner he says, "I was sent only to the lost sheep of the house of Israel." Ignoring this rather gentle dismissal, she simply gasps, with tears flowing down her cheeks, "Lord, help me." In previous stories, such a heartfelt request always moves Jesus to action.

But not this time. Jesus counters that "[i]t is not fair to take the children's food and throw it to the dogs." We know from other stories that Jesus has often addressed the needs of non-Jews without hesitation. The hero of one of his best stories, the Good Samaritan, is a non-Jew. So why does he insult this Canaanite woman? The simplest explanation is just as with all human beings—and he *was* one, after all—he's having a tough day, and he's not at his best. He doesn't feel like helping this foreign person and has provided a perfectly good rationalization for why he doesn't have to.

But this woman is not only insistent, she is quick on her feet. "Yes, Lord, yet even the dogs eat the crumbs that fall from their masters' table!" Touché! This is impressive—her retort is the sort of thing that I always come up with hours after the conversation is over and I'm alone. The unnamed woman is able to match Jesus one-liner for one-liner with her daughter's health, perhaps her life, at stake. And it works. Something—her persistence, her intelligence, her lack of regard for propriety—cuts through Jesus's resistance. "Woman, great is your faith. Let it be done for you as you wish." And her daughter was healed instantly. Jesus and his followers continue on their way, and we never hear of this woman again.

Without the exchange between Jesus and the woman, this tale would be indistinguishable from dozens of other accounts of persons healed by Jesus. Why does the author choose to tell the story in this fashion? Why make a point of showing that even Jesus had off days, could be rude and judgmental, and occasionally had feet of clay just as we all do? In addition to driving home the "Jesus was a human being" point, a point that the Nicene Creed reminds Christians of every Sunday but that we tend to ignore, there's a more direct behavioral lesson to be learned here.

Jesus listened. Even on a bad day crowded with distractions and annoyances, he was able to hear the truth, recognize he was being less than his best self, and do better. We all have bad days, undoubtedly many more than Jesus did, and we tend to use "I was having a bad day" as a justification for all manner of bad behavior, even to those we love the most. The story of Jesus having a bad day lets us know not only that the best of us occasionally fail to live up to expectations, but also that such failures need not be debilitating. Each of us can hear the truth and change a bad day into a not-so-bad one. Even the Son of God.

For reflection: Does it surprise you that Jesus showed himself to be human in such an obvious way? What difference does this make to your faith journey?

Proper 16: This teaching is difficult

Year B: John 6:56–69

In the Proper 16 Year B reading from John's gospel, a number of Jesus's followers complain after one of his teachings that "this teaching is difficult; who can accept it?" When Jesus responds with a few more of his patented cryptic remarks, "many of his disciples turned back and no longer went about with him."

These frustrated former disciples have a point. I might have gone with them. The lesson is indeed a difficult one, including the claim that only those who drink Jesus's blood and eat his flesh will have eternal life. But this is by no means the only difficult lesson that they've heard from Jesus. From selling all you have being a prerequisite for following him, and letting your enemy strike both sides of your face while giving him your cloak to go with the coat he stole, to letting the dead bury the dead and hating your father and mother if you want to be his disciple, Jesus is full of difficult teachings.

Small wonder that Christians, generally lacking the courage to simply walk away, tend to water down and systematize the radical elements of the gospel into manageable directives. These reduced commands require behaviors and commitments that, although burdensome at times, can be carried out by any reasonably dedicated and sincere adult. For many of us, "this teaching is difficult; who can accept it?" is not really a question of understanding at all. For we understand the hard sayings all too well, and conclude that they are just too much.

In October of 2006, the news of a shooting in an Amish schoolhouse in Nickel Mines, Pennsylvania, burst onto the nightly news. A neighborhood milkman carrying a small arsenal of weapons walked into the school and started shooting, killing five and wounding many more before turning his gun on himself. In the midst of deep grief, the interconnectedness of the Amish community was demonstrated through comprehensive mutual support and, most shockingly, immediate forgiveness.

At a prayer service the night after the shootings, a local pastor reported that he was in the kitchen of the shooter's family home when an Amish neighbor came by. "He wrapped his arms around the gunman's dad for an hour. He said, 'We will forgive you.'" The pastor's conclusion: "God met us in that kitchen."

For several years, I included this tragic event and its aftermath as the central part of the midterm exam in my General Ethics class. I provided my students with a newspaper account of the Amish community's reaction to the shootings, then asked them to try to make sense of what happened within the parameters of the moral frameworks we had studied during the first half of the semester. They couldn't do it.

Furthermore, many of my mostly parochial school–educated students found something twisted, even offensive, in the willingness of the Amish community to forgive the murderer of their children. Comments ranged from "this is completely abnormal" to "these people are sick." Yet one member of the Amish community included in the article said: "Our faith tells us to act like Christ did on his way to the cross."

Once shortly after reading my midterms, I was having a beer with a colleague at the local watering hole on Friday afternoon, unwinding from the week. I described the reactions of my students to the behavior of the Amish. In response, my colleague said, "I also am shocked by what the Amish did, but I don't know why. As a Christian, I should be shocked that I'm shocked. They are just doing what Jesus said to do."

As someone who has grappled with issues of Christian faith from my youth, my own temptation is to think of the Amish as über-Christians, somehow capable of moral heroics that normal persons such as I can only admire from a distance and not even aspire to. That rationale is particularly tempting because I, like many mainstream Christians, have been encouraged to think that it is the priests, pastors, monks, nuns, and missionaries who are the elite corps of Christians, freeing me to reduce expectations considerably.

But Jesus's call to take up my cross and follow him does not contain a loophole or room for an amendment. Which brings me back to the beginning—"this teaching is difficult." I can't love my neighbor as myself. I can't love God more than I love Jeanne. I can't sell all that I have, give the proceeds to the poor, and follow Jesus. It's too hard, and I've grown tired of pretending that a lukewarm, watered-down version is sufficient. Maybe I'm one of those who identify with the remaining disciples who asked, "Lord, to whom can we go? You have the words of eternal life." So, where does that leave me? I want to follow. I can't follow.

A still small voice offers a bit of hope. "Of course it's too hard. Of course, you can't do any of these things. That's the point. I can, and I am in you." If divine love has indeed overcome the world, then perhaps it can even overcome me.

For reflection: Which of Jesus's teachings do you find most difficult in your faith walk? What are your strategies for addressing this difficulty?

Proper 17: Moving past tradition

Year B: Deuteronomy 4:1–2, 6–9; Mark 7:1–8, 14–15, 21–23

In the Proper 17 Year B reading from Mark's gospel, we find the Pharisees once again getting in Jesus's face, this time because they have observed his disciples "eating with defiled hands, that is, without washing them." Jesus's response to their criticism—"there is nothing outside a person that by going in can defile, but the things that come out are what defile"—raises many important questions, including the role of tradition and accepted practice in a living and dynamic faith.

It is easy to immediately identify the Pharisees in the Gospels as the "bad guys," continually criticizing Jesus and his followers and, ultimately, at least partially responsible for Jesus's arrest, conviction, and execution. Equally important to remember is that the Pharisees were the religious authorities of Jesus's world, the persons who both knew the rules of Jewish law and prescribed behavior backward and forward. They at least claimed to follow those rules to the letter. And they had Scripture and verse to back them up.

Today's reading from Deuteronomy in the Jewish Scriptures is a case in point:

> *So now, Israel, give heed to the statutes and ordinances that I am teaching you to observe, so that you may live to enter and occupy the land that the LORD, the God of your ancestors, is giving you . . . You must observe them diligently, for this will show your wisdom and discernment to the peoples, who, when they hear all these statutes, will say, "Surely this great nation is a wise and discerning people."*

To be a faithful Jew is to live according to the rules, sometimes very detailed, in the Torah. The rules about ritual handwashing that the Pharisees accuse Jesus's disciples of ignoring are not mere suggestions—obedience to them defines being a faithful

Jew. Dietary and cleanliness rules and traditions are not optional. According to the traditional parameters of Judaism, the Pharisees are correct.

Which makes Jesus's response to the Pharisees even more radical than it might first appear. Jesus's radical claim is that the right relationship with God is not about externals, but rather about the heart. In Mark's Gospel, Jesus tells the Pharisees that

> *Isaiah prophesied rightly about you hypocrites, as it is written, 'This people honors me with their lips, but their hearts are far from me; in vain do they worship me, teaching human precepts as doctrines.' You abandon the commandment of God and hold to human tradition.*

Philosophers have argued for centuries over which element of moral decision-making is more important: *what* one does or *why* one does it? The reason or intention behind one's action or the actual thing one did? The Pharisees and Jesus are on opposite sides of this debate.

The Pharisees argue that one's righteousness and right standing with God depend on what one does. In favor of this claim is that one's behavior is something that can be observed by others, as evidenced by the Pharisees' calling out Jesus's disciples for not abiding by traditional cleanliness requirements. These are community standards that everyone is required to abide by; the Pharisees, as keepers of the law, are the ultimate judges and authorities of whether one's behavior is acceptable.

But as Jesus points out in today's gospel, one could be flawless in one's obedience to behavioral rules and yet have a heart infected with "fornication, theft, murder, adultery, avarice, wickedness, deceit, licentiousness, envy, slander, pride, and folly." As we read in 1 Samuel, humans "look on the outward appearance, but the Lord looks on the heart." In other words, God is far less interested in what a person does as with the intentions behind what that person does.

This should not have been a surprise to the Pharisees and other religious authorities, since the Jewish Scriptures are full of passages where God makes clear that external sacrifices pale in comparison to the state of one's heart and soul. But in the tradition that Jesus was born into and is part of, right standing with God and one's community are one and the same with faithful carrying out of traditional practices and norms.

It is worth noting that there is also a downside to focusing morality and righteousness on intentions rather than actions. While actions can be observed and judged or rewarded collectively because they are on public display, one's intentions are subjective and private. No one knows what my intentions are unless I tell them—and there's no guarantee that I'll tell the truth. Jesus has moved one's relationship with God from external to internal, from performance to intention and conscience. It's a radical move—no wonder the Pharisees were (and still are) upset.

For reflection: Take a position on which matters more—what one does or why one does it. What are the strengths and problems of both perspectives?

Proper 18: Like a tree

Year C: Psalm 1

In Psalm 1, the appointed psalm for Proper 18 Year C, the righteous are described as being "like trees planted by streams of water . . . in all that they do, they prosper." We can learn a great deal about spiritual health and growth from trees.

There are two kinds of living things, distinguished by the strategies they have developed in response to perceived threat and danger. One kind responds to danger by running away from it, developing strategies and evolving tools to sidestep threats in more and more complex and sophisticated ways. We call this kind of living thing Animals.

The other kind's strategy is to hunker down, grow roots along with protective armor, and face danger by refusing to be moved. We call this kind of living thing Plants. We human beings tend to consider our animal capacities to choose between various strategies as one of our most important and wonderful abilities, going so far as defining "freedom" in terms of how many options we have to choose from. But the older I get, the more I think that the nature of true freedom is a lot more like the strategy of plants.

In *The Cruelest Month*, the third of Louise Penny's Inspector Gamache mystery series, the good inspector has a conversation with Gilles Sandon, one of more than a half-dozen suspects in the most recent murder in Three Pines, Quebec. Sandon is a former lumberjack, a hulking brute of a guy with an unexpected sensitive side.

Gilles tells Gamache of a day a number of years ago when he walked with his tree-cutting colleagues into the woods for a day of work and heard a whimpering that sounded like a baby animal. As the whimpering became louder and turned into a cry, then a scream, Gilles realized that this wasn't an animal sound at all. Furthermore, none of his companions could hear it.

> *Something had changed overnight. I'd changed. I could hear the trees. I think I could always hear their happiness. I think that's why I felt so happy myself in the forest. But now I could hear their terror too ... Mostly trees are quiet. Just want to be left alone. Funny how I learned about freedom from creatures that are rooted in place.*

Gilles's life was changed, beginning with his understandably being fired from his lumberjacking job (if a lumberjack won't cut trees, what's the point?). Over time, he became a woodworking artist, specializing in making chairs out of dead trees that he carefully selects after they have fallen; as Gamache says, Gilles makes his living giving dead trees new life.

In our American culture, freedom is often thought of as the ability to do whatever I want, whenever I want to do it, free from the interference of anyone other than me. Any perceived limitation on what I want to do, even if clearly in my own interest and that of others, is a violation of my "freedom." But philosophers have argued for centuries that this uninhibited throwing around of my deliberative weight is anything but true freedom.

Iris Murdoch argues in *The Sovereignty of Good* that it is in the small choices concerning what we pay attention to and adopt as centrally important that true freedom is to be found:

> *But if we consider what the work of attention is like, how continuously it goes on, and how imperceptibly it builds up structures of value round about us, we shall not be surprised that at crucial moments of choice most of the business of choosing is already over. This . . . implies that the exercise of our freedom is a small piecemeal business which goes on all the time and not a grandiose leaping about unimpeded at important moments.*

True freedom, under this description, is to act in attunement with one's character and conscience—items that are constructed slowly, deliberately, and in accord with one's best nature. A lot like a tree, in other words.

A human being can never entirely trade its animal survival strategies for the rootedness of a plant. But we can, as Gilles, learn a lot about freedom and how to be in the world from a tree. I used to wonder what Martin Luther meant when, at the Diet of Worms, he concluded his refusal to recant his heretical writings by saying, "Here I stand. I can do no other." Of course, he could have done otherwise! I would complain. No one is forcing him not to recant.

But Luther's point was that at this stage of his life, recanting his writings would be the same as ceasing to be Martin Luther.

He can do no other because his character has rooted him in place. As Murdoch suggests, if one has paid attention to the incremental tiny choices that shape one's character and life over time, what to do at "crucial moments of choice" will not only be clear—it will be unavoidable. Be like a tree.

For reflection: Psalm 1 tells us that the righteous "yield their fruit in its season, and their leaves do not wither." Are there times in your faith journey where patience and rootedness have produced fruit?

Proper 19: Radical forgiveness

Year A: Genesis 50:15–21; Matthew 18:21–35

The Proper 19 Year A readings from the Jewish Scriptures and Matthew's gospel are stories about radical forgiveness. The last chapter of Genesis concludes the story of Joseph and his brothers; the brothers are afraid that after their father's death, Joseph will exact revenge for being sold into slavery many years earlier. In Matthew, Peter expects Jesus to provide a limit to how often he must forgive someone who has sinned against him. Both Joseph's brothers and Peter find their expectations to be entirely wrong.

The Year A readings from the Jewish Scriptures have followed the Joseph saga for several weeks, beginning with Proper 14. Joseph is the eleventh and favorite son of Jacob, the first child of Jacob's beloved wife Rachel. For any number of reasons, Joseph is intensely disliked by his older brothers—they first throw him into a well, then sell him to some traders who in turn sell him as a slave in Egypt to an important court official. Joseph's brothers tell their father that his favorite has died.

Joseph's story over the final chapters of Genesis tracks his path from slave to the most powerful man in Egypt other than the Pharoah, a rise fueled by luck, Joseph's gift for dream interpretation, and his clearly being favored by God. When famine strikes years later and Jacob sends his sons to Egypt to purchase grain, they have no idea that the Egyptian official they have to negotiate with is none other than the brother whom they sold into slavery so long ago. He recognizes them, though, and clearly enjoys yanking their collective chain and making their lives miserable for a few chapters.

But ultimately, "Joseph could no longer control himself," and he reveals his true identity to his shocked and dismayed brothers. Joseph has every reason to use his power as a tool of vengeance and retribution against his brothers, but in an act of radical forgiveness he sends them home in order to bring Jacob and rest of the family to Egypt, where the elderly Jacob will benefit from Joseph's love and live out the rest of his days.

When Jacob finally dies, the older brothers are afraid that Joseph's forgiveness was an act of respect for his father; now that Jacob is gone, Joseph might finally use his power to exact retribution. They offer themselves to him as slaves; in response he says, "Do not be afraid! Am I in the place of God? Even though you intended to do harm to me, God intended it for good." In the coming decades the Israelites prosper in Egypt and multiply in numbers and strength until "a new king arose over Egypt, who did not know Joseph."

One wonders if Joseph would have been as forgiving of his brothers if he had still been a slave when he encountered them years after they sold him into slavery. Forgiveness seems more possible from a lofty perch where he holds all the cards and they can no longer harm him. But the prayer that Jesus teaches his disciples makes it clear that unconditional forgiveness is a prerequisite for those who seek right relationship with God and to follow Jesus. Radical and unlimited forgiveness is to be offered to those who have wronged us, no matter who they are or what they have done.

When Peter asks Jesus about how far forgiveness is to extend in scope and frequency, he clearly has a specific issue in mind.

He's not asking about forgiveness in general, but in essence is asking, "How often do I need to forgive a person from our insider group who has wronged me?" In Season Four of *The Chosen*, Peter specifically has Matthew in mind as the one who has wronged him, a former tax collector who almost cost Peter his livelihood and his freedom before Jesus called him out of his tax-collecting booth with a simple "Follow me." We can almost hear the attitude in Peter's voice when he asks, "Seven times?"

Jesus's answer—"seventy-seven times"—takes forgiveness out of the realm of the humanly possible and places it squarely in the realm of the miraculous. Only a thoroughly transformed person can offer unlimited forgiveness. But then, being transformed is what following Jesus is all about.

For reflection: We often say, "I'll forgive, but I won't forget," as if forgiveness and forgetting that one has been wronged are two different things. But does the sort of forgiveness that Jesus is speaking about leave the door open for the wronged person to remember what the forgiven person did? Why or why not?

Proper 20: The last will be first

Year A: Matthew 20:1–16

The gospel reading from Matthew for Proper 20 Year A is one of my favorite New Testament passages to discuss with first-semester freshmen. Jesus says that "the Kingdom of Heaven is like" a landowner who pays everyone the same daily wage no matter how long they have worked. My students bristle at his apparently cavalier attitude toward the rule that people should be paid in proportion to the amount of work that they do, an assumption so ingrained in our Western, Protestant-work-ethic, capitalist ethos that any apparent violation is close to an economic crime. "This guy sounds like a socialist!" several of my students complain, and they have a point.

The situation described has a very contemporary feel to it. People out of work gather at an agreed location, hoping that they will be one of the few picked when bosses with work available arrive at the crack of dawn. Those looking for work might not have proper documentation—whatever their situation, they are not blessed with the security of regular employment. The landowner or his representative arrives at dawn, offers the handful selected to work an agreed-upon wage for their day of labor, while those who are not selected are left unemployed for yet another day. But the harvest is ready to be gathered, and the owner returns every three hours, at 9:00 a.m., at noon, and at 3:00 p.m., hiring more workers each time. Even at 5:00 p.m., a few more are grabbed from the marketplace to help make a final push in grape-harvesting for the last hour of the workday.

Things get weird at the end of the day, as the landowner pays all of the workers, starting with those hired last, the same amount of money, no matter how long they worked. Is it because, as my students suspect, he is a proto-socialist? No, as is clear when he responds to the complaining laborers who have worked all day and have just been paid the same amount of money paid to the one-hour people,

> *Friend, I am doing you no wrong; did you not agree with me for the usual daily wage? Take what belongs to you and go; I choose to give to this last the same as I give to you. Am I not allowed to do what I choose with what belongs to me?*

In the landowner's world, contracts mean something. This is what we agreed to—this is what is going to happen. And in the landowner's world, the profits from his vineyard are not common property—they are *his* property. He's a first-century capitalist, in other words.

So, why does he distribute wages in such a non-capitalistic way? In the Kingdom of Heaven, the kingdom that it is the responsibility of all who profess to follow Jesus to establish on earth now, familiar rules are not eliminated. Rather, they are transformed. With Kingdom-of-Heaven eyes, the landowner sees something more important than profit—he sees that at the foundational level, everyone shares the same needs. A daily wage is meant to meet daily needs—and each person has these needs regardless of how long they work. The landowner never asks why those he hires were unemployed, nor does he ask why some of them were not available for work until late in the day. These details simply do not matter.

What does matter is that each of the workers at the end of the day needs the same things, and the landowner satisfies those needs with his own money. Those who worked all day believed they deserved more than those who came late. In the eyes of the landowner, all deserve a daily wage because all have the same needs. Our expectations are turned upside-down once again. But that's how things work in the Kingdom of Heaven. The more you have, the more opportunities you have to give it away.

Recall the prophet Micah's directive that we are to do justice, love mercy, and walk humbly with God. The landowner embodies all three elements of Micah's directive. He embodies humility because, although the profits from the vineyard belong to him, he understands that everything we have is a gift and that the only possible response to such generosity is to channel the generosity outward. He knows that justice is never spread equally over talents, wealth, abilities, or anything else, but rather it is our responsibility to create a world in which all human needs are responded to equally, regardless of which humans have the needs. Finally, he is merciful because he sees his laborers not as replaceable cogs in the money-making machinery, but as fellow human beings with whom, at least for this day, he can share his abundance willingly and liberally. For as Jesus concludes his parable, "[T]he last will be first, and the first will be last."

For reflection: In an earlier gospel story, Jesus observes that "you cannot serve God and money." What might it mean to be wealthy but not to be in service to wealth?

Proper 21: Delegating authority

Year B: Numbers 11:4–6, 10–16, 24–29; Mark 9:38–50

The Proper 21 Year B reading from the Jewish Scriptures is from Numbers. We find the liberated Israelites in the desert, and they are complaining—again. God has miraculously provided them with a daily supply of manna to keep them from starving, but everyone is pining for the wonderful variety of food they remember eating in Egypt.

> *We remember the fish we used to eat in Egypt for nothing, the cucumbers, the melons, the leeks, the onions, and the garlic; but now our strength is dried up, and there is nothing at all but this manna to look at.*

Of course, they have conveniently forgotten that when they were in Egypt they were *slaves*. God is understandably annoyed, and so is Moses. But Moses's annoyance isn't just with this rabble of complainers he is in charge of; he's had it up to here with God as well.

Moses is tired of being the recipient of Israelite complaints when he's not the one who put them in this situation. He needs help.

> *I am not able to carry all this people alone, for they are too heavy for me. If this is the way you are going to treat me, put me to death at once—if I have found favor in your sight— and do not let me see my misery.*

In response to Moses's complaint, God suggests that Moses take some of his power and authority and distribute it among some carefully selected folks so they can share the burden of leadership and responsibility. Moses selects seventy guys he trusts, brings them to the tent of meeting, God empowers the seventy men in response to which they start "prophesying," and a solid chain of command and power sharing structure is established.

We learn a few things about delegating authority from this passage. First, authority and power appear to be zero sum, meaning that empowering others automatically means that the leader is disempowered to that same extent. Only secure people should be in leadership roles, in other words. Second, power needs to be distributed carefully, publicly, and according to recognizable procedures. Finally, others need to be clearly made aware of the new power structure. The "prophesying" part of the story means, at the very least, that the newly empowered have been publicly marked as such. Secretly adding layers of bureaucracy without transparency is a recipe for suspicion and resentment.

This all sounds eminently sensible—until problems arise in the next few verses. It turns out that two of the guys selected by Moses for empowerment didn't make it to the tent of meeting, but they start prophesying in the camp as if they had participated in the official empowerment ceremony. In other words, they are acting with authority without having been officially empowered. Moses's number one assistant, Joshua, tells Moses about the two guys and asks for permission to stop the unauthorized activity of these pretenders.

Surprisingly, Moses tells Joshua to leave them alone. "Are you jealous for my sake? Would that all the Lord's people were prophets, and that the Lord would put his spirit upon them." In the short span of one story authority has shifted from one person to the vision of a projected future in which anyone who has the vision and ability to be effective can act on it. What about the hierarchy? What about keeping tight control on how power is distributed? Is this any way to run an organization?

Apparently it is, because in the gospel reading for the day from Mark similar issues arise. Jesus has empowered his disciples to preach the gospel, cast out demons, and heal the sick. Then John reports some disturbing news to Jesus: "Teacher, we saw someone casting out demons in your name, and we tried to stop him, because he was not following us." The disciples assume that only those specifically authorized and empowered by Jesus to do special stuff should be doing it. This stranger using Jesus's name to cast out demons is guilty of spiritual plagiarism, in other words. But just as Moses told Joshua, Jesus tells John and the rest to leave this guy alone. "Whoever is not against us is for us."

As we often learn when reading stories about the intersection of the human and the divine, things divine operate according to entirely different rules than those to which we are accustomed. Or perhaps according to no recognizable rules at all. The divine spirit is frequently likened to the wind, which blows where it wants when it wants, without regard to our expectations, desires, or weather predictions. The takeaway? Divine power and authority are *not* a zero sum game. They can and will show up in all sorts of unlikely places, even those we have not authorized. Especially in those places.

For reflection: What do the stories from Numbers and Mark tell us about our human attempts to organize and control? Why are such attempts guaranteed to "quench the Spirit"?

Proper 22: Jesus and children

Year B: Mark 10:2–16

In the Proper 20 Year B gospel from Mark 9, Jesus picks up a child and says, "Whoever welcomes one such child in my name welcomes me, and whoever welcomes me welcomes not me but the one who sent me." This is one of the few times we see Jesus interacting with children in the Gospels; today's Proper 22 Year

B reading is another. We know little about the lives of any of the disciples, including whether any of them had children, but in today's reading, it is clear they believe Jesus has far more important things to do than hanging out with kids. As people bring their children to Jesus for a blessing, the disciples turn them away. Jesus is not amused.

Let the little children come to me; do not stop them; for it is to such as these that the Kingdom of God belongs. Truly I tell you, whoever does not receive the kingdom of God as a little child will never enter it.

Artists' renditions of this scene invariably depict Jesus sitting on a rock with a half dozen innocent looking children around three to five years old gathered around him. Jesus usually is holding in his lap the youngest of the children, who is reaching up with a chubby hand to touch Jesus's beard.

What might it mean to receive the Kingdom of God as a little child? A typical interpretation is that we must turn to God with the innocence of a child—unquestioning, accepting, vulnerable, and passive. Yet anyone who has ever spent time with a small child or even an infant for more than a few minutes knows that this is a romanticized and surface-level picture. Children are far more interesting and complicated than can be captured by "innocent."

Augustine of Hippo, the fourth-century theologian and philosopher who is second only to the Apostle Paul in his influence on the development of early Christian doctrine and belief, spends a good deal of time at the beginning of his *Confessions* pushing back against the popular myth that infants are innocent creatures. *Confessions* is a classic story of conversion; Augustine spends the first half of the book convincing the reader that he (and therefore we) are self-centered and power hungry, steeped in sin, from the moment we emerge from the womb.

From his own observation of infants, Augustine imagines what he was like as an infant.

> *For an infant of that age, could it be reckoned good to use tears in trying to obtain what it would have been harmful to get, to be vehemently indignant at the refusals of free and older people . . . who would not yield to my whims, and to attempt to strike them and to do as much injury as possible?*

As Hannah Arendt famously quipped, "Every generation, civilization is invaded by tiny barbarians—we call them 'children.'"

Aristotle opened one of his magisterial books with the observation that "philosophy begins in wonder"—a natural capacity that all human beings are born with and that we lose in short order under the pressures of conformity, education, and constant demands of behavior and belief. I often tell students in my introductory classes that it is this capacity of wonder that I hope to reawaken in each of them. Wonder is what a baby shows with her frank and forthright way of gazing about in bewilderment, trying to balance her oversized head on her undersized neck as she wonders, "What's this thing? And what's that over there? And good God, what's THAT??" An inexhaustible openness to everything, an amazement in which nothing is mundane and everything is new.

It is this sense of amazement and wonder that Jesus has in mind when he says that we must receive the Kingdom of God "as a little child." The disciples (and we) are regularly confused and bewildered by what Jesus says concerning the Kingdom of God because little of what he says makes sense when viewed through familiar and traditional lenses. Paul writes that "if anyone is in Christ, there is a new creation: everything old has passed away; see, everything has become new." For the young child, there is no "everything old"—everything by definition is new.

The greatest source of wonder and amazement in the Kingdom of God is that, despite our flaws, imperfections, self-obsession, and dark sides, we are the subjects of radical divine love. The first and greatest thing that a child needs to grow and thrive is an abundance of love, something each new human being has an unlimited capacity to receive. And in the Kingdom of God, an unlimited supply of unconditional love is available.

For reflection: What are the characteristics of your inner child that make it possible to receive the Kingdom of heaven?

Proper 23: An inconvenient faith

Year B: Mark 10:17–31

The Proper 23 Year B gospel is a familiar story in which Jesus once again makes clear that the cost of following him is far greater than many might be willing to pay. A wealthy young man approaches Jesus and asks, "What must I do to inherit eternal life?" Their ensuing conversation reveals that following Jesus is more than an inconvenience—it requires everything.

"Sorry for the inconvenience" has over the years become the "go to" comment in student-to-professor emails when the communication contains information that the student doesn't want to take responsibility for. "I will be missing the two classes before Thanksgiving because my plane ticket home for the holiday is on Sunday. Sorry for the inconvenience." "I'm going to need an extension on the paper due Friday because I have another paper due that day. Sorry for the inconvenience." They invariably discover that the inconvenience is theirs, not mine.

Human beings do not like being inconvenienced. Although we might not admit it, we love "convenience stores" and have made them a ubiquitous part of the American landscape, simply because they are "convenient." All of which makes Jesus' conversation with the wealthy young man problematic. In response to the man's question about inheriting eternal life, Jesus answers that the young man knows very well what to do—he should keep the commandments, listing a few for the guy just in case he had forgotten them. In Jesus's Jewish culture, right relationship with God requires obedience to the commandments and rules, something that, although inconvenient is doable for a committed person.

But the conversation takes a deeper turn when the young man replies, "Teacher, I have kept all these from my youth." He's not looking for general affirmation from Jesus; he's already past the point of thinking that simply following the rules is good enough, or he wouldn't have asked in the first place. The young man is looking for more. Jesus answers, "Go, sell what you own, and give the money to the poor, and you will have treasure in heaven; then come, follow me." We also all know the end of the story—"He was shocked and went away grieving, for he had many possessions." For the wealthy young man, this is far more than inconvenient. It is impossible.

What precedes Jesus's shocking challenge is very interesting. Mark says that "Jesus, looking at him, loved him." This is a man who wants more, Jesus knows it, and Jesus loves him for it. But central to the gospel message is a disturbing truth—the thing that you cannot do will be the thing that is required. And it will be something different for each of us. This story isn't primarily about the incompatibility of wealth and following Jesus. It's a story about being called to come and die. The God of love is not a cure for anything. The God of love is the greatest dispenser of inconvenience and worse. "I have not come to bring peace, but a sword," and this is a sword that cuts deepest in those who are the most obsessed with knowing God.

The Gospels contain "hard sayings" that run roughshod over our desire that our dealings with what is greater than us be similar to a convenience store transaction. "What do I need to do in order for X to happen, in order for Y not to happen, in order for Z to get a break?" are the sorts of questions we so often want answered, but they are always the wrong sort of question when directed toward the transcendent.

I once heard the poet Michael Dennis Browne speak of an insight that unexpectedly came to him as he grieved the tragic death of his younger sister, a woman for whom family and friends had gone hoarse with their prayers and petitions for healing. And she died anyways. Browne said, "It came to me that this is not a God who intervenes, but one who indwells." That changes everything. The inconvenience of trying to believe in a God who never calls, writes, or tweets is transformed into the challenge of being God in the world.

For reflection: Which of Jesus's many difficult sayings in the Gospels do you find most challenging? What do you do when confronted by it?

All Saints Sunday: How to become a saint

Year A: Revelation 7:9–17; Year B: Revelation 21:1–6

November 1 is All Saints' Day; when it falls on a weekday, All Saints is frequently celebrated on the first Sunday of November. Singing the hymn "For all the saints" is a must; readings for the day from Revelation provide visions of "a new heaven and earth" in which countless throngs of saints and angels worship continuously before the throne of God.

I come from a hardcore Protestant world in which we did not do saints. Even though I have spent much of my adult life, first as a graduate student, then as a professor, as a non-Catholic in Catholic higher education, I am still somewhat confused by and uncomfortable with the very notion of "sainthood." In Albert Camus's novel *The Plague*, one of the main characters, when described as a "saint" by another character, responds that "sanctity doesn't really appeal to me . . . What interests me is being a man." I agree with that sentiment. What makes a person a saint? Is there such a thing? Is there a difference between sainthood and moral excellence? Is sainthood a reasonable goal for a human life, or is it something one stumbles into?

A recurring character in Louise Penny's Inspector Gamache series of mysteries raises the saint issue in an interesting way. Dr. Vincent Gilbert abandoned a lucrative medical career to live in and care for a community of people with Down syndrome. Based on that experience he wrote a book called *Being*, by all accounts a memoir of staggering honesty and humility.

Dr. Gilbert abandoned his family to enter this community, walking back into their lives years later to find that his alienated son and wife want nothing to do with him. Dr. Gilbert is temperamental, a contrarian by nature, very full of and in love with himself, and is generally disliked by everyone in town. These contradictions have earned him the title "The A**hole Saint" among his family and acquaintances who know and don't love him.

In *Bury Your Dead*, Vincent is living in a cabin deep in the Québec woods because his family refuses to have him at their hotel and spa in town. Inspector Beauvoir, another recurring character in the series who is recovering from serious gunshot wounds received a few weeks earlier, finds himself in the cabin after Vincent rescues him from a snowmobile mishap. As Vincent tenderly cares for the feverish Beauvoir, the inspector compares his current situation to his previous medical care over the past weeks.

> *He'd been touched by any number of medical men and women. All skilled personnel, all well intentioned, some kind, some rough. All made it clear they wanted him to live, but none had made him feel that his life was precious, was worth saving, was worth something . . . [Vincent's] healing went beyond the flesh, beyond the blood. Beyond the bones.*

The ability to recognize the value and dignity in another person, regardless of their status or situation, is one of the hallmarks of a healer—and perhaps a saint.

Less than a page after Inspector Beauvoir's observations about Vincent's healing abilities, the men enjoy a meal together while listening to a hockey game on the radio. Before long Vincent says something judgmental and nasty about Beauvoir's culinary preferences, as much in character as Vincent's tender care a page earlier. "The a**hole was back," Beauvoir notes. "Or, more likely, had been there all along in deceptively easy company with the saint."

When Camus's character in *The Plague* says that he is more interested in being a man than in being a saint, he might be drawing a false distinction. Saintliness does not require rising above one's humanity or leaving it behind; rather, sainthood is entirely compatible with being human—warts and all. Raising saints to the level of veneration removes them from the daily human grind and places them beyond the reach of reasonable human aspiration.

It is good to know that Thomas Aquinas had an eating disorder and that Mother Teresa of Calcutta could be a pain in the butt and was hard to get along with, because such information reminds us that saints are human beings. Taking it a notch higher, being reminded of Jesus's divinity immediately causes me to think about his humanity—warts and all (yes, I suspect Jesus had warts). The excellence that sainthood represents is a matter of being fully human. Each of us can learn to see another person as more than a problem to be avoided or solved, to be attentive to the other in the manner that their humanity deserves. Each of us can learn to be healers, in other words—even if we still occasionally are a**holes. That's what incarnation is all about.

For reflection: Is sainthood something a person of faith should aspire to, or is it something that is a byproduct of committing one's life to Christ?

Proper 25: Prosper the work of our hands

Year A: Psalm 90:1–6, 13–17

One of the few remaining vestiges of my Baptist upbringing, one that I will carry with me until I die, is my love of traditional hymns. We sang them with gusto in four parts in our little church, accompanied by my mother on an out-of-tune upright piano. I first learned to appreciate poetry through the lyrics of these old Protestant standards, learning far more about Christian belief and doctrine from their eighteenth- and nineteenth-century authors than anything I ever heard from the pulpit.

One Sunday when I was pinch-hitting at the organ, the processional hymn was one of my favorites: "O God, Our Help In Ages Past" by Isaac Watts. It has a great bass line, and it's a lot of fun to play. It was also the entrance hymn at the September 14, 2001, National Prayer Service at the National Cathedral in Washington, DC, three days after the 9/11 terrorist attacks. It puts tears in my eyes every time.

Watts's hymn is a setting of Psalm 90, one of the Psalm options for Ordinary Time 22 Year A. The older I get, the more meaningful two of the later verses in the hymn become:

> *A thousand ages in thy sight*
> *Are like an evening gone,*
> *Short as the watch that ends the night*
> *Before the rising sun.*
> *Time, like an ever-rolling stream,*
> *Bears all our years away;*
> *They fly forgotten, as a dream*
> *Dies at the opening day.*

Psalm 90 establishes unflinchingly a truth that most of us would just as soon ignore. We are all going to die. In addition to reminding us of our mortality, the Psalmist explores another inescapable truth: God is God, and you're not. God is eternal, and you're not. No punches are pulled. Verses 5 and 6: "You sweep them away; they are like a dream, like grass that is renewed in the morning; in the morning it flourishes and is renewed; in the evening it fades and withers." Verse 10: "The days of our life are seventy years, or perhaps eighty, if we are strong; even then their span is only toil and trouble; they are soon gone, and we fly away."

True, but certainly not comforting. Existentialist atheists Jean-Paul Sartre or Albert Camus could have written verse 12: "So teach us to count our days that we may gain a wise heart." On a bad day, none of this sounds any better than "Life's a bitch and then you die." I am reminded of what an eighty-something-year-old Benedictine monk (now over 100 years old) once told me several years ago as we walked slowly together across the green to noon prayer at the abbey where he had spent more than six decades. "Vance, sabbatical is God's best idea. And getting old is God's worst idea."

When I introduce the existentialists in various classes, my students often wonder why Sartre, de Beauvoir, Camus, and others are so morbid and obsessed with death. My response is that they are trying to counter our human conviction that we are immortal. Oh, we don't say that, but we live our lives as if we have all the time in the world, as if we will never die. We "know" that we are short-term creatures, that we have a shockingly short shelf life, but we don't want to think or hear about it.

Although Isaac Watts's setting of Psalm 90 asks God to be "our shelter from the stormy blast, and our eternal home," the psalm itself says nothing about eternal life or bliss in heaven. That's a New Testament concept. And to be honest, I'm not attracted to the idea that this life is just practice for eternity, even though that often seemed to be the only reason to be a Christian in my youth.

Perhaps I'm too influenced by the existentialists—I want to live my life at least trying to stay conscious of being a short-term creature. And at the end of Psalm 90, the psalmist provides the proper daily attitude focus, with just a hint of wishful thinking thrown in:

> *Satisfy us in the morning with your steadfast love,*
> *So that we may rejoice and be glad all our days.*
> *Make us glad as many days as you have afflicted us,*
> *And as many years as we have seen evil.*
> *Let your work be manifest to your servants,*
> *And your glorious power to their children.*
> *Let the favor of the Lord our God be upon us;*
> *And prosper for us the work of our hands—*
> *O prosper the work of our hands.*

There's no guarantee that joy and affliction will balance out at the end of my life. But rejoicing is a verb and a choice, even for a short-term creature.

For reflection: The ancient Stoics had a famous saying: "Carpe diem" (seize the day). How does this saying compare to the message of Psalm 90?

Proper 26: Wherever you go

Year B: Ruth 1:1–18

The Proper 26 Year B reading from the Jewish Scriptures is the opening verses of the Book of Ruth, a brief gem squeezed between the historical books of Judges and 1 Samuel. I always assign it when we are in Old Testament week in the interdisciplinary program I teach in, for several reasons.

First, it is brief enough to be read in one sitting. More important, it is unique among the books of the Jewish Scriptures because the main characters are women and God never makes an appearance. No miracles, no divine insecurity, or meddling with the lives of human beings. Ruth is a story of normal human beings trying to live their lives with integrity and care in the middle of a world that is both challenging and unfair. Sounds a lot like the world we live in.

Ruth is set during the time of the judges, the decades between the Israelite occupation of the Promised Land and the events leading up to the kingship of Saul and David. It is a time of political instability during which the various tribes of Israel, in very loose confederation, stake out territory and frequently must defend themselves against attacks from various indigenous groups they had displaced. Ruth tells a story that is as contemporary as today's headlines—a story of people migrating from their native land in search of better lives.

During a time of famine, an Israelite family migrates to Moab to the southeast due to rumors that there is food there. Even though Jewish law prohibits an Israelite from marrying a non-Israelite, Naomi's sons marry Moabite women—Ruth and Orpah. But then disaster strikes—both of Naomi's sons and her husband die and she finds herself a widow with two widowed non-Jewish daughters-in-law.

Naomi advises her daughters-in-law to return to their families while she, her life in many respects over as an older woman with no male to protect her, will return to her own homeland. Orpah sadly does so, but Ruth refuses to leave, telling Naomi, "Where you go, I will go; where you lodge, I will lodge; your people shall be my people, and your God my God." For many years, a musical setting of this text was standard fare at wedding ceremonies, but these words are not about the love between people committing to marriage. Rather, they are an expression of a young woman's love for an older woman whom she cannot bear to leave, even for the best of reasons.

The story of Ruth and Naomi continues in the Proper 27 Year B reading from the Jewish Scriptures. Back in her homeland, Naomi relies on her considerable intelligence and powers of manipulation to worm her way into the orbit of Boaz, a relative of her deceased husband, on whose support she has a distant claim, according to the law. Wisely, she uses the youthful and beautiful foreigner Ruth to draw Boaz's attention, first as Ruth works in his fields, then in the following passage:

> *Naomi her mother-in-law said to her, "My daughter, I need to seek some security for you, so that it may be well with you. Now here is our kinsman Boaz... See, he is winnowing barley tonight at the threshing floor. Now wash and anoint yourself, and put on your best clothes and go down to the threshing floor... When he lies down, observe the place where he lies; then, go and uncover his feet and lie down; and he will tell you what to do."*

I have heard many ministers fumble around with this portion of the story, but my eighteen-year-old freshmen know exactly what's going on. Naomi is telling Ruth to seduce Boaz. And it works—Boaz does tell Ruth "what to do," they soon marry, and their son, Jesse, is the father of David, the shepherd who becomes king of Israel and whose descendant will be Jesus himself.

A few takeaways from Ruth's story: First, the divine likes to work outside the box. Including the foreigner Ruth, as well as the prostitute Rahab (Boaz's mother) from the Book of Joshua, in the royal bloodline is a violation of God's own law—and God doesn't seem to care. Second, Naomi never waited for a "word from God" to decide the best path forward. She relied instead on her own knowledge, intuition, cunning, good nature, and ability to work the system to her advantage. Third, God frequently doesn't say anything—that does not get the person of faith off the hook of responsibility for her or his own life. Sometimes you make the best choices you can and trust that God is there. Finally, women clearly are better than men at working their way out of seemingly impossible situations.

For reflection: Concerning God's will, Archbishop Desmond Tutu once said in a documentary, "There is no shaft of light that comes from heaven and says to you 'Okay, my son or my daughter, you are right.' You have to hold on to it by the skin of your teeth and hope that there's going to be vindication on the other side." Does this ring true?

Proper 27: Where to find me

Year B: Psalm 146; Mark 12:38–44

The Proper 27 Year B gospel reading from Mark draws our attention to the importance of using what one has to further the Kingdom of God rather than asking, "I'm only one person—what can I do?" It is story of the widow whose meagre two-coin offering is declared by Jesus to be far better than the greater amounts of money that others gave, simply because the widow gave "everything she had."

Throughout season two of *The Chosen*, Jesus's notoriety continues to grow; about halfway through the season, Jesus asks the disciples to help him plan for a "big sermon" that he intends to give soon. Some of the disciples are assigned crowd control (they are expecting thousands of people), while others are tasked with finding the perfect location for the event. Flyers are written and distributed throughout the towns around the Sea of Galilee. Jesus asks Matthew, who has been taking notes on everything that has happened since he was called to follow Jesus some months earlier, to be his sounding board and provide critical input as he works through multiple drafts of the sermon.

By the time we reach the final episode of the season, the sermon's content is set—except for the beginning. Writers and speech givers know that often the introduction is written last—Jesus goes off by himself overnight to consider and pray. At dawn he awakens Matthew and says, "I've got it . . . a map. Directions where people should look to find me."

The Beatitudes follow; as Jesus blesses the poor in spirit, those who mourn, those who hunger and thirst for righteousness, the merciful, the pure in heart, the peacemakers, and the persecuted, the camera cuts to scenes of various disciples and followers who exemplify each category in Jesus's introduction. When Jesus is finished with the blessings, with tears in his eyes Matthew asks, "How is it a map?" Jesus replies, "If someone wants to find me, these are the groups they should look for."

Psalm 146, one of the psalm options for Proper 27 Year B, expresses a similar sentiment. I learned to love the psalms as I spent several sabbatical months at morning, noon, and evening prayer with dozens of Benedictine monks; the psalms are the spine of their daily office. Over a few weeks one cycles through all of the 150 psalms, expressions of every human emotion imaginable as we seek to connect with what is greater than us. Writing a letter from prison to his parents two years before his death, Dietrich Bonhoeffer answered their question of how he spent the endless hours of nothingness in prison. "I read the Psalms every day, as I have done for years; I know them and love them more than any other book."

The final entries in the collection of 150 psalms are praises of various sorts—noon prayers at St. John's Abbey in Minnesota, the place where I first learned to inhabit these ancient poems, include one of the final five psalms in rotation. I always looked forward to Psalm 146, which summarizes what God cares about the most:

> *It is the Lord who keeps faith forever,*
> *Who executes justice for the oppressed; who gives bread to*
>   *the hungry.*
> *The Lord sets the prisoners free; the Lord opens the eyes of*
>   *the blind.*
> *The Lord lifts up those who are bowed down; the Lord loves*
>   *the righteous.*

> *The Lord watches over the strangers; he upholds the orphan and the widow.*

As Jesus says to Matthew in *The Chosen*, these are the types of people one should look for if one is looking to find God.

All of which serves to make sense of Jesus's imagining of the Last Judgment in Matthew's gospel, one of the many passages in the Gospels that turns all of our traditional expectations on their head. When the Son of Man invites those on his right hand "to inherit the kingdom prepared for you from the foundation of the world," because they attended to him when he was hungry, thirsty, a stranger, naked, sick, and imprisoned, those on his right hand are confused. "When did we do any of these things?" they ask. "Just as you did it to one of the least of these who are members of my family, you did it to me." Where to find Jesus could not be more clear.

For reflection: *Where are the places where you most frequently find Jesus? Who are the people in whom you find him present most clearly?*

Proper 28: A different voice

Year B: 1 Samuel 1:4–20, 2:1–10

The books of the Bible were written over centuries by men in patriarchal societies; the texts were selected and curated in later centuries by men in patriarchal societies. And yet, women's voices frequently shine through, as we have seen throughout this book. Sarah, Rahab, Naomi, Ruth, Elizabeth, Mary . . . and in the Proper 28 Year B reading from the Jewish Scriptures, Hannah.

First Samuel begins with a tale that contains many familiar elements from the narratives in the Jewish Scriptures: a powerful and faithful woman surrounded by mansplaining and clueless males who, although in social positions of power, have a lot to learn. Hannah is the favored (and presumably younger) wife of Elkanah, a faithful man of the tribe of Ephraim. Peninnah, Elkanah's other wife, has several children, while Hannah has no children because "the Lord had closed her womb." In a typically human move, Peninnah uses Hannah's barrenness against her; the text reports that Peninnah "used to provoke her severely, to irritate her" to the point that Hannah "wept and would not eat."

We've seen this story before—think, for instance, of Sarah's jealousy when Hagar gives birth to Abraham's son Ishmael while the son promised Abraham and Sarah has noticeably not shown up. Or of Rachel, the beautiful and favored wife of Jacob, who has no reason to be jealous of her less beautiful, older sister Leah—whom Jacob does not love but had to marry in order to marry Rachel—except that Rachel has no children and Leah has many children.

In Hannah's case, well-meaning but totally clueless Elkanah doesn't help the situation when he mansplains to Hannah why, in truth, she has no reason to be sad. He asks, "Hannah, why do you weep? Why do you not eat? Why is your heart sad? Am I not more to you than ten sons?" Using a bit of imagination, I suspect that Hannah's unrecorded response was along the lines of, "No, dear, as a matter of fact, you *don't* mean more than ten sons to me. In this patriarchal iron age world where a woman's worth is calculated by how many sons she has, you definitely are not worth even one son, let alone ten. You want to know how to help? Get Peninnah off my back!" Or something like that.

One year at Shiloh, the holy place where Elkanah and the family travelled annually to sacrifice and worship, Hannah went off by herself and, "weeping bitterly," begged God for a son, promising to dedicate that son to God should her prayer be heard and answered. She prayed silently, but her lips were moving. Enter another well-meaning but clueless male. Eli, the priest in charge at Shiloh, concluded that this weeping and mumbling woman was drunk. "How long will you make a spectacle of yourself?" Eli asked. "Put away your wine."

The Hannah of my imagination, sick to death of male obtuseness and mansplaining, thinks, "Oh for God's sake, old man, leave me alone! The Lord and I are trying to have a conversation here! Get out of my face!" Showing great self-control instead, Hannah says,

> *I am a woman deeply troubled; I have drunk neither wine nor strong drink, but I have been pouring out my soul before the Lord. Do not regard your servant as a worthless woman, for I have been speaking out of my great anxiety and vexation all this time.*

Eli, to his credit, realizes his mistake and wishes her well—but wisely doesn't guarantee anything.

We learn subsequently that Hannah does become pregnant, her son Samuel is dedicated to the Lord as she promised (which means that Eli ends up being his father figure and unofficial mentor in things concerning the divine), becoming a major player in the events that move the Jewish people from a loose tribal confederation to a fledgling nation. Samuel, acting as the representative of God in these events, anoints Saul, then David, as the first two kings of Israel.

Hannah gets center stage one last time in the next chapter with "Hannah's Prayer," a powerful song of thanksgiving, prophecy, and justice that Mary, the mother of Jesus, clearly had in mind when she sings her similarly powerful Magnificat of thanks centuries later. We would do well to embrace the grace and power of Hannah, this apparently insignificant woman who simply wanted to be treated fairly and to be a mother.

> *The bows of the mighty are broken, but the feeble gird on strength.*
> *Those who were full have hired themselves out for bread,*

but those who were hungry are fat with spoil . . .
The Lord kills and brings to life; he brings down to Sheol
  and raises up.
The Lord makes poor and makes rich; he brings low, he also
  exalts.
He raises up the poor from the dust; he lifts the needy from
  the ash heap,
to make them sit with princes and inherit a seat of honor.

Let it be so.

For reflection: Which of the many women in the Bible have been most meaningful to you in your faith journey? Why?

Proper 29: The reign of Christ

Year A: Matthew 25:31–46; Year B: John 18:33–37; Year C: Luke 23:33–43.

Proper 29, the last Sunday of Ordinary Time, is "The Reign of Christ" Sunday. The gospel options vary considerably, including the sheep and goats passage in Matthew 25, Jesus's trial before Pilate in John 18, and the crucifixion in Luke 23. Taken together, they provide a range of responses to Pilate's question, "Are you a king?"

Perhaps the greatest confusion among those who heard and followed Jesus during his time on earth was directly related to Pilate's question. For the people of an occupied land, it is no wonder that they had expected the Messiah to be a liberator. As the men on the road to Emmaus said, "We had hoped that he was the one to redeem Israel." John and James ask if they might have the special favor of sitting on either side of his throne in his glory—it is clear that they are not thinking of some distant future. Two thousand years later, the notion of fusing religious belief with political power continues to be persistent and seductive.

Jesus responds to Pilate's "Are you the king of the Jews?" as he often does by asking a question himself. "Do you ask this on your own, or did others tell you about me?" The first possibility means that Pilate is concerned about a threat to Caesar's authority, while the second reveals Jesus's suspicion that Pilate is being pressured by others, namely the Jewish religious authorities. In the complex politics of an occupied land, the Jewish authorities want Jesus gone, but need to convince the occupying Romans that it is in their best interest to convict and execute Jesus.

Once Pilate makes clear that it is the Jewish authorities that Jesus is in trouble with, Jesus puts his cards on the table.

My kingdom is not from this world. If my kingdom were from this world, my followers would be fighting to keep me from being handed over to the Jews. But as it is, my kingdom is not from here.

In other words, if I was the sort of king you are thinking about, we wouldn't be having this conversation. But my kingdom is not about political power at all. There's something completely different going on.

In the religious world of my youth, we were consistently told that Christians are *in* this world but are not to be *of* this world. I took that to mean that we are stuck here in this physical way station for a certain amount of years until we get to go to heaven. In the meantime, don't be seduced by anything your physical reality has to offer. This may have just been a product of my youth, but my sense was that the adults thought this way as well.

I always resisted this directive because I sort of liked this world. But Jesus's teachings and parables about the Kingdom of heaven make clear that it is not something to be imagined in a projected future. Recall his metaphors about our roles in the Kingdom of Heaven. We are salt, yeast, a mustard seed ... all tiny, insignificant, embedded things that facilitate great change over time. The Kingdom of heaven changes everything from the inside rather than imposing change from the outside. We are *in* the world but not *of* the world because by being followers of Jesus, we are agents of change in the world.

Remember the ruler in Kierkegaard's story of the king and the maiden. He makes a true relationship with the maiden possible not through an expression of his power, but by voluntarily setting that power aside in humility and becoming as she is. That is the kind of king that Jesus is and what the Spirit inspires in us, as Paul captures in this passage from Philippians:

> *Who, though he was in the form of God*
> *Did not regard equality with God as something to be exploited,*
> *But emptied himself, taking the form of a slave,*
> *Being born in human likeness.*
> *And being found in human form, he humbled himself*
> *And became obedient to the point of death—*
> *Even death on a cross.*

The passage closes with a description of an exalted Son, tying together the humble and royal aspects of kingship.

> *Therefore God also highly exalted him and gave him the name*
> *That is above every name,*
> *So that at the name of Jesus every knee should bend*
> *In heaven and on earth and under the earth*
> *And every tongue should confess that Jesus Christ is Lord.*

For reflection: Which metaphor is more meaningful in your faith journey, the exalted Jesus or the servant Jesus?

Postlude: Peace be to you

As the liturgical cycle returns to Advent of another year, I return to one final memory from the early months of my immersion into liturgical worship. Charles Harlan Clarke was the organist and choirmaster during the 1980s at St. Matthew's Episcopal Cathedral in Laramie, Wyoming, where during my late twenties I was earning my master's degree at the University of Wyoming. The cathedral's music ministry was of higher quality than one might expect in the middle of a sparsely populated 7500-foot-high desert. Charles was glad to welcome me into his circle of musicians; soon I was playing the grand piano in the corner of the sanctuary on Sunday mornings as Charles played the beautiful organ that, when it was constructed in the early twentieth century, was the largest organ west of the Mississippi.

One of the choir's favorite choral works was Paul Manz's "E'en So Lord Jesus, Quickly Come," a favorite because it was sung a capella (meaning that I could leave the piano and join the choir) and fit the mix of voices in our collection of singers perfectly. It was particularly a favorite piece because of the story behind its composition. Charles was friends with Paul Manz, a renowned composer and organist, and loved to tell us the tale as Manz had told it to him.

Manz and his wife, Ruth, often were a composing team for choral music, with Ruth writing the lyrics and Paul the music. At Christmas time in 1953, their three-year-old son was gravely ill; Paul and Ruth kept vigil at his hospital bedside as his doctors and nurses gently prepared them for their son's inevitable death. Late one evening, Ruth remembered some verses from the book of Revelation that suddenly took on new meaning as their son lay dying. She worked with the text a bit and showed it to her husband. After adapting verses from the beginning of Revelation for the body of the lyrics, she closed with this meditation on the final verses of the book.

> *E'en so, Lord Jesus, quickly come, / And night shall be no more; / they need no light nor lamp nor sun, / For Christ will be their all.*

In an interview fifty years later, Ruth Manz told an NPR interviewer that "I think we'd reached the point where we felt that time was certainly running out so we committed it to the Lord and said, 'Lord Jesus quickly come.'"

As Charles told the story, the medical staff finally convinced Ruth and Paul to go home to get a bit of sleep, promising that they would be contacted immediately if there was any change in their son's condition. In the middle of the night the phone rang—it was the hospital. "Your son has woken up—his fever has broken. The doctor on staff has checked him out carefully and he appears to be fine. You can come and take him home."

Every time the choir sang this piece, someone in the choir was designated to tell the story of how it came to be written before we sang it. As far as I can remember, no one ever made it through the story without choking up; we finally had the story printed up and placed in the bulletin each time we performed it. It is Paul Manz's best-known work—over one million copies have been sold. We live in a world that sorely needs light to shine into the darkness and hope to replace despair—miracles do happen. Peace be to you.

Notes

Many of the books cited below are available in several editions and translations. I have cited the editions that have been most useful to me over the years.

All quotations from the Bible are from the New Revised Standard Version (NRSV) unless otherwise specified. The NRSV is the translation used in the Revised Common Lectionary.

Prelude and Preliminaries

A new hymnal ... *Episcopal Hymnal 1982* (Church Publishing, 1985).

Book of Common Prayer ... 1979 Book of Common Prayer (Church Publishing, 1979).

The challenge of sacred texts

The letter kills ... 2 Corinthians 3:6.

The basics

Revised Common Lectionary ... The Revised Common Lectionary was released in 1994 after a nine-year trial period. It is the product of a collaboration between the conference of Catholic bishops in both the United States and Canada and many traditionally liturgical Protestant churches, including Lutheran, Anglican (Episcopal), Presbyterian, and (some) Methodist. The lectionary can be found at https://lectionary.library.vanderbilt.edu/.

Before we begin . . .

The number of weird and wondrous happenings . . . Sarah Bessey, *Field Notes from the Wilderness* (Convergent, 2024).

Chapter 1: Advent—What May We Hope For?

What can I know? . . . Immanuel Kant asks these questions in *The Critique of Pure Reason* (Hackett, 1996).

First Sunday of Advent: Keep awake!

They shall beat their swords into plowshares . . . Isaiah 2:4 (Year A).

The Son of Man is coming . . . Matthew 24:44 (Year A).

They will see the Son of Man coming . . . Mark 13:26–33 (Year B).

It is now the moment . . . Romans 13:11 (Year A).

But about that day and hour no one knows . . . Matthew 24:40–42 (Year A).

You know what time it is . . . Romans 13:11–12 (Year A).

Second Sunday of Advent: Prepare the way

The Baptist's miraculous birth . . . Luke 1:5–24; 57–66.

And you, child, will be called . . . Luke 1:76–79

Søren Kierkegaard tells a lovely story about a powerful king . . . Søren Kierkegaard, *Philosophical Fragments* (Princeton, 1985).

Third Sunday of Advent: The Lord is with you

What good is it for me that Christ was born . . . Meister Eckhart, *Meister Eckhart: Selections from His Essential Writings* (HarperCollins, 2005).

Greetings, favored one! The Lord is with you . . . Mary's Magnificat is in Luke 1:46–55 (Year A), also included in the Year B and C readings for the Fourth Sunday of Advent. The story of the Annunciation is told in Luke 1:26–38, the Year B gospel reading for Advent 4.

Some terrible aboriginal calamity . . . John Henry Newman, *Apologia pro Vita Sua* (Penguin, 1995).

Fourth Sunday of Advent:
The strong and silent type

A genealogy that traces Jesus's ancestry . . . Matthew 1:1–17.

They wind up in Jericho . . . The story of the spies and Rahab is found in Joshua 2:1–16.

Chapter 2: Christmas Season—
God Made into Flesh
Christmas Day: What really happened?

We read the same facts differently . . . William James, "Pragmatism and Humanism," in *Pragmatism and Other Writings* (Penguin, 2000).

Wise men following a star . . . Matthew 2:10–12.

Christmas Day: Putting skin on

This is the story I will wrestle with . . . Rachel Held Evans, *Inspired* (Thomas Nelson, 2018).

The virgin birth is something that happens within us . . . Meister Eckhart, *Meister Eckhart: Selections from His Essential Writings*

The last thing any of us needs . . . Barbara Brown Taylor, *An Altar in the World* (HarperOne, 2010).

The First Sunday After Christmas Day:
"In the beginning was the Word"

There is a mystery in reading . . . Simone Weil, *Simone Weil: Late Philosophical Writings* (Notre Dame, 2015).

Your words were found and I ate them . . . Jeremiah 15:16.

I only read what I am hungry for at the moment . . . Simone Weil, *Waiting for God* (HarperPerennial, 1973).

The Second Sunday After Christmas Day:
Jesus goes about His Father's business

Save his people from their sins . . . Matthew 1:21.

Chapter 3: Epiphany—Jesus's Coming Out Party
Epiphany of the Lord

The voice of the LORD flashes forth flames of fire . . . Psalm 29:7–9 (Epiphany 1, Year A).

He will not cry or lift up his voice . . . Isaiah 42:2–3 (Epiphany 1, Year A).

Those who are unhappy have no need . . . Simone Weil, "Reflections on the Right Use of School Studies with a View to the Love of God," in *Waiting for God*.

I am the LORD, I have called you in righteousness . . . Isaiah 42:6–9 (Epiphany 1, Year A).

First Sunday After Epiphany—
The baptism of Jesus

Iris Murdoch's novel *Nuns and Soldiers* . . . Iris Murdoch, *Nuns and Soldiers* (Penguin, 2002).

Second Sunday After Epiphany—
The wedding at Cana

> **Grace means you're in a different universe** . . . Anne Lamott, *Plan B: Further Thoughts on Faith* (Riverhead, 2006).

Third Sunday After Epiphany:
"Today . . . in your hearing"

> **The opposite of faith is not doubt, but certainty** . . . All passages from Anne Lamott in this section are from *Plan B*.
>
> **[h]aving made the world** . . . Joan Chittister, *Joan Chittister: Essential Writings* (Orbis, 2013).

Fifth Sunday After Epiphany:
The light of the world

> **"Solar" and "lunar" spirituality** . . . Barbara Brown Taylor, *Learning to Walk in the Dark* (HarperOne, 2014).
>
> **Call to me and I will answer you** . . . Jeremiah 33:3.
>
> **Pray without ceasing** . . . 1 Thessalonians 5:17
>
> **Whatever things are true . . . honest** . . . Philippians 4:8

Seventh Sunday After Epiphany:
"Be perfect"

> **What of the command** . . . Iris Murdoch, *The Sovereignty of Good* (Routledge, 2001).
>
> **The central structural pillars** . . . Iris Murdoch, *The Bell* (Penguin, 2001).
>
> **Perfect love casts out fear** . . . 1 John 4:18.

Eighth Sunday After Epiphany: "Consider the lilies"

Anne Lamott tells the story of an older woman . . . Anne Lamott, *Almost Everything* (Riverhead Books, 2018).

Teach us to care . . . T. S. Eliot, *The Waste Land and Other Poems* (Signet, 1998).

Rilke said of Cezanne that he did not paint . . . Iris Murdoch, "On 'God' and 'Good,'" in *Existentialists and Mystics* (Penguin Books, 1999).

I will call this to mind . . . Lamentations 3:21–26.

Transfiguration Sunday: "Listen to Him"

The newly crowned King David . . . 2 Samuel 6:1–8.

"The Great Stone Face" . . . Nathaniel Hawthorne's short story "The Great Stone Face" is widely anthologized in collections of American short fiction.

Man is the creature who makes pictures of himself . . . Iris Murdoch, "Metaphysics and Ethics" in *Existentialists and Mystics*.

To look and to eat are two different things . . . Simone Weil, *First and Last Notebooks* (Wipf and Stock, 2013).

Chapter 4: Lent—Beauty for Ashes
Ash Wednesday: "To dust you shall return"

The only trouble is that in the spiritual life . . . Thomas Merton, *Contemplative Prayer* (Image, 1971).

A penitential psalm attributed to David . . . The story of David, Bathsheba, and Nathan is told in 2 Samuel 11–12.

Create in me a clean heart . . . Psalm 51:10–12, 17.

A man after [God's] own heart . . . 1 Samuel 13:14.

First Sunday in Lent: Temptation

Fyodor Dostoevsky's tale of the Grand Inquisitor... Fyodor Dostoevsky, *The Brothers Karamazov* (Picador, 2021).

When Christ calls a man, he bids him come and die... Dietrich Bonhoeffer, *The Cost of Discipleship* (Touchstone, 1995).

Second Sunday in Lent: "God so loved the world."

From the book of Numbers... Numbers 21:4–9. This is the Lent 4 Year B lectionary reading from the Jewish Scriptures.

Paul and Silas are miraculously released... Acts 16:16–34.

Third Sunday in Lent: Wells of water

These are waterless springs... 2 Peter 2:17.

My thoughts are not your thoughts... Isaiah 55:8–9.

Fourth Sunday in Lent: The prodigal son

A small theology classic... J. B. Phillips, *Your God Is Too Small* (Touchstone, 2004).

Fifth Sunday in Lent: The raising of Lazarus

When Christ calls a man... Dietrich Bonhoeffer, *The Cost of Discipleship*.

They alone will see God... Simone Weil, "The Love of God and Affliction," in *Waiting for God*.

Die before you die. C. S. Lewis, *Letters of C. S. Lewis* (HarperOne, 2017).

Chapter 5: Holy Week—
From Hosanna to Sepulcher
Palm Sunday: From palms to Passion

What do we really believe? . . . Dietrich Bonhoeffer, *Letters and Papers from Prison* (Fortress, 2014).

Monday of Holy Week: "You always have the poor"

The accounts in Matthew's and Mark's gospels . . . Matthew 26:6–13; Mark 14:3–9

Tuesday of Holy Week: Righteous Anger

Cleanse the temple . . . Matthew 21:12–13; Luke 19:45–46. A similar story is told in John's gospel (John 2:13–16), but it is placed early in Jesus's ministry rather than during Holy Week.

Jesus cursed a fig tree . . . Matthew 21:18–22; Mark 11:12–14.

The prophet Micah . . . Micah 6:8.

The intimation of a great reality . . . Marilynne Robinson, "Grace," in *The Givenness of Things* (Picador, 2015).

Suddenly you are in a different universe . . . Anne Lamott, *Small Victories: Spotting Improbable Moments of Grace*.

Wednesday of Holy Week: Betrayal or Denial?

Before the cock crows . . . John 13:38.

Kate Bowler's recent book . . . Kate Bowler with Jessica Ritchie, *Good Enough: 40ish Devotionals for a Life of Imperfection* (Convergent, 2022).

"Cheap" and "costly grace" . . . Dietrich Bonhoeffer, *The Cost of Discipleship*.

The golden calf narrative . . . Exodus 32:1–35.

Maundy Thursday: "Could you not keep awake one hour?"

Jesus heads to the Garden of Gethsemane . . . Matthew 26:35–45, Mark 14:32–42; Luke, 22:39–46.

Jesus asked in Gethsemane . . . Dietrich Bonhoeffer, *Letters and Papers from Prison*.

The extreme greatness of Christianity . . . Simone Weil, *Gravity and Grace* (Routledge, 2002).

Good Friday: Actually, He died

The end of the book of Job . . . Job 42:10–17.

If Christ be not raised, your faith is vain . . . 1 Corinthians 15:14.

Holy Saturday: "Mortals die, and are laid low"

Resurrection is a fiction and a distraction . . . Christian Wiman, *My Bright Abyss* (FSG Adult, 2014).

Supposing that the disciples . . . Fyodor Dostoevsky, *The Idiot* (Vintage, 2003).

If God did not exist, it would be necessary to invent him . . . This was one of Voltaire's favorite aphorisms, found frequently in his letters and published work.

If we ask our Father for bread, he will not give us a stone. Simone Weil, "Reflections on the Right Use of School Studies with a View to the Love of God," *Waiting for God*

I know that my redeemer liveth . . . Job 19:25–26; 1 Corinthians 15:20, King James Version.

A myth is a story that you know is true . . . Kathleen Norris, *Amazing Grace: A Vocabulary of Faith* (Riverhead, 1999).

Chapter 6: Easter Season— Everything Has Changed

Easter people living in . . . Barabara Johnson, *Splashes of Joy in the Cesspools of Life* (Thomas Nelson, 1996).

No cure for being human . . . Kate Bowler, *No Cure for Being Human* (Random House, 2022).

Easter: Now it begins

The lectionary gospel readings for Easter Sunday . . . John 20:1–18; Matthew 28:1–10 (Year A); Mark 16:1–8 (Year B); Luke 24:1–12 (Year C).

I will sing and make melody . . . Psalm 57:8–9.

Easter: Getting Jesus out of the tomb

. . . differ radically depending upon what one believes happened at Easter . . . Marcus Borg and N.T. Wright, *The Meaning of Jesus* (HarperOne, 2007).

An Easter interview with CNN . . . "The Easter story helps an 'outcast' preacher find her way back home" CNN US 4/25/19. https://www.cnn.com/2019/04/21/us/outcast-pastor-finds-way-home-easter/index.html

Second Sunday of Easter: A doubting disciple

There is no hostility so extreme . . . Montaigne, "Apology for Raymond Sebond," in *The Complete Essays of Montaigne* (Stanford, 1958).

There is no use our mounting on stilts . . . Montaigne, "Of experience," in *The Complete Essays of Montaigne*.

Doubt and dedication . . . Annie Dillard, *For the Time Being* (Vintage, 2000).

Third Sunday of Easter: "We had hoped"

Now faith, hope, and love abide . . . 1 Corinthians 13:13.

Does it ever surprise you that God chooses . . . Kathleen Norris, *Amazing Grace*.

Fourth Sunday of Easter: The good shepherd

I am the good shepherd . . . John 10:11 (Year B).

A tender-hearted shepherd . . . Matthew 18:10–14.

Even though I walk through the darkest valley . . . Psalm 23:4.

Sixth Sunday of Easter: "Do you want to be made well?"

Those who are unhappy have no need for anything . . . Simone Weil, "Reflections on the Right Use of School Studies with a View to the Love of God," in *Waiting for God*.

Ascension Sunday: Passing the baton

Day unto day takes up the story . . . Psalm 19:2.

Pentecost: "The rush of a violent wind"

Have this treasure in clay jars . . . 2 Corinthians 4:7.

There is no longer Jew or Greek . . . Galatians 3:28–29.

Trinity Sunday: Celebrating life

The most beautiful of lives to my liking . . . Michel de Montaigne, "Of experience," in *Essays*.

Her finely touched spirit had still its fine issues . . . George Eliot, *Middlemarch* (Penguin, 2003).

Chapter 7: Ordinary Time—Parables and Miracles

The Sundays of Ordinary Time are organized according to "Propers." A Proper is a collection of prayers and lessons tied to secular calendar dates from late May until late November, when Advent begins. There are 29 Propers; Proper 29 is always the last Sunday before Advent. Since the date of Easter varies from year to year, the Proper of the first Sunday of Ordinary Time in a given liturgical year ranges from Proper 4 to Proper 8. On the rare occasion Easter is so early that Proper 1, 2, or 3 is scheduled, the readings for those Propers are the same as Epiphany 6, 7, or 8 of that same liturgical year.

Proper 4: Do I matter?

The eternal silence of these infinite spaces . . . Blaise Pascal, *Penseés* (Penguin, 1995).

The wonderful books of Dr. Seuss . . . Theodore Seuss Geisel (Dr. Seuss), *Horton Hears a Who* (Random House, 2020).

Proper 5: Follow me

We know the truth . . . Blaise Pascal, *Penseés*.

There are more things . . . William Shakespeare, *Hamlet* Act 1, Scene 5.

Whether he is a sinner . . . John 9:25.

Proper 6: The fruit of the spirit

The one who began a good work . . . Philippians 1:6.

Proper 7: Jesus and family values

Let the dead bury their own dead . . . Luke 9:60 (Proper 8 Year C).

Woman, what concern is that to you? . . . John 2:4.

Should we encourage twelve-year-olds . . . Luke 2:41–52.

I will show you . . . 1 Corinthians 12:31.

Proper 8: The fertility of silence

Anne Lamott quotes a friend . . . Anne Lamott, *Bird by Bird* (Vintage, 1995).

Surely the Lord is in this place . . . Genesis 28:16.

Silence reminds me . . . Kathleen Norris, *Amazing Grace*.

I have calmed and quieted my soul . . . Psalm 131:2.

Proper 9: Blessed with a burden

The light of the world . . . Matthew 5:14.

Proper 10: The Good Samaritan

The prophet Micah's directive . . . Micah 6:8.

We live in a dream . . . Iris Murdoch, "Above the Gods," *Existentialists and Mystics*.

The extremely difficult realization . . . Iris Murdoch, "The Sublime and the Good," *Existentialists and Mystics*.

Proper 11: Sowing and reaping

My thoughts are not your thoughts . . . Isaiah 55:8–9.

Not only did the creator create everything . . . Annie Dillard, *Pilgrim at Tinker Creek* (HarperPerennial, 2003).

Properly speaking, God does not make . . . Pierre Teilhard de Chardin, *Christianity and Evolution* (Harcourt, 1974).

God is not the puppet master . . . quoted in Krista Tippett, *Speaking of Faith* (Penguin, 2008).

There is grandeur in this view of life . . . Charles Darwin, *The Origin of Species* (Barnes and Noble, 2004).

Proper 12: The kingdom of heaven is like . . .

A parable is a metaphor or simile . . . C. H. Dodd, *The Parables of the Kingdom* (Nisbet, 1946).

Proper 13: Feeding the five thousand

The stories of miracles complicate everything . . . Simone Weil, *Gravity and Grace*.

The earth is charged . . . "God's Grandeur," in *Gerard Manley Hopkins: The Major Works* (Oxford, 2009).

Wherever you turn your eyes . . . Marilynne Robinson, *Gilead* (Picador, 2004).

Proper 14: Walking on water

Mark's account . . . Mark 6:45–52.

Proper 17: Moving past tradition

Isaiah prophesied rightly . . . Isaiah 29:13.

As we read in 1 Samuel . . . 1 Samuel 6:17.

Proper 18: Like a tree

Something had changed overnight . . . Louise Penny, *The Cruelest Month* (Minotaur, 2011).

But if we consider what the work . . . Iris Murdoch, *The Sovereignty of Good*.

Proper 19: Radical forgiveness

The Joseph saga . . . Genesis 37:1–4, 12–28.

Joseph could no longer control himself . . . Genesis 45:1.

A new king arose over Egypt . . . Exodus 1:8.

Proper 20: The last will be first

You cannot serve God and money . . . Matthew 6:24.

Proper 22: Jesus and children

Proper 20 Year B gospel . . . Mark 9:30–37.

The beginning of his classic *Confessions* . . . Augustine of Hippo, *Confessions* (Oxford, 1991).

Philosophy begins in wonder . . . Aristotle, *Metaphysics* (Hackett, 2016).

If anyone is in Christ . . . 2 Corinthians 5:17.

Proper 23: An inconvenient faith

I have not come to bring peace . . . Matthew 10:34.

All Saints Sunday: How to become a saint

Albert Camus's novel . . . Albert Camus, *The Plague* (Knopf Doubleday, 1991).

He'd been touched by any number . . . Louise Penny, *Bury Your Dead* (Minotaur, 2011).

Proper 26: Wherever you go

The story of Ruth and Naomi continues . . . Ruth 3:1–5.

Proper 27: Where to find me

I read the psalms every day . . . Dietrich Bonhoeffer, *Letters and Papers from Prison*.

The last judgment in Matthew . . . Matthew 25:31–46.

Proper 29: The reign of Christ

We had hoped that he was the one . . . Luke 24:21.

John and James . . . Mark 10:34.

This passage from Philippians . . . Philippians 2:6–11. This poetic expression is thought to be a passage from an early Christian hymn.

Postlude

Some verses from the book of Revelation . . . Revelation 1:4–8, 22:20.

For Further Reading

The resources listed here are all referenced in this book; they are just some of the eclectic texts that have been helpful companions in my faith journey.

Aristotle. *Metaphysics* (Hackett, 2016).
Augustine of Hippo. *Confessions* (Oxford, 1991).
Bessey, Sarah. *Field Notes from the Wilderness* (Convergent, 2024).
Bonhoeffer, Dietrich. *The Cost of Discipleship* (Touchstone, 1995).
———. *Letters and Papers from Prison* (Fortress, 2014).
Borg, Marcus, and N. T. Wright. *The Meaning of Jesus* (HarperOne, 2007).
Bowler, Kate. *No Cure for Being Human* (Random House, 2022).
Bowler, Kate, and Jessica Ritchie. *Good Enough: 40ish Devotionals for a Life of Imperfection* (Convergent, 2022).
Camus, Albert. *The Plague* (Knopf Doubleday, 1991).
Chittister, Joan. *Joan Chittister: Essential Writings* (Orbis, 2013).
Darwin, Charles. *The Origin of Species* (Barnes and Noble, 2004).
Dillard, Annie. *For the Time Being* (Vintage, 2000).
———. *Holy the Firm* (HarperPerennial, 2003).
———. *Pilgrim at Tinker Creek* (HarperPerennial, 2003).
Dodd, C. H. *The Parables of the Kingdom* (Nisbet, 1946).
Dostoevsky, Fyodor. *The Brothers Karamazov* (Picador, 2021).
———. *The Idiot* (Vintage, 2003).
Eckhart, Meister. *Meister Eckhart: Selections from His Essential Writings* (HarperCollins, 2005).
Eliot, George. *Middlemarch* (Penguin, 2003).
Eliot, T. S. *The Waste Land and Other Poems* (Signet, 1998).
Evans, Rachel Held. *Inspired* (Thomas Nelson, 2018).
Geisel, Theodore Seuss (Dr. Seuss). *Horton Hears a Who* (Random House, 2020).

James, William. *Pragmatism and Other Writings* (Penguin, 2000).
Johnson, Barbara. *Splashes of Joy in the Cesspools of Life* (Thomas Nelson, 1996).
Kant, Immanuel. *The Critique of Pure Reason* (Hackett, 1996).
Kierkegaard, Søren. *Philosophical Fragments* (Princeton, 1985).
Lamott, Anne. *Almost Everything* (Riverhead, 2018).
____. *Bird by Bird* (Vintage, 1995).
____. *Plan B: Further Thoughts on Faith* (Riverhead, 2006).
____. *Small Victories: Spotting Improbable Moments of Grace* (Riverhead, 2014).
Lewis, C. S. *Letters of C. S. Lewis* (HarperOne, 2017).
Merton, Thomas. *Contemplative Prayer* (Image, 1971).
Montaigne, Michel de. *The Complete Essays of Montaigne* (Stanford, 1958).
Murdoch, Iris. *The Bell* (Penguin, 2001).
____. *Existentialists and Mystics* (Penguin Books, 1999).
____. *Nuns and Soldiers* (Penguin, 2002).
____. *The Sovereignty of Good* (Routledge, 2001).
Newman, John Henry. *Apologia pro Vita Sua* (Penguin, 1995).
Norris, Kathleen. *Amazing Grace: A Vocabulary of Faith* (Riverhead, 1999).
Pascal, Blaise. *Penseés* (Penguin, 1995).
Penny, Louise. *The Cruelest Month* (Minotaur, 2008)
____. *Bury Your Dead* (Minotaur, 2011).
Phillips, J. B. *Your God Is Too Small* (Touchstone, 2004).
Robinson, Marilynne. *Gilead* (Picador, 2004).
____. *The Givenness of Things* (Picador, 2015).
Taylor, Barbara Brown. *An Altar in the World* (HarperOne, 2010).
____. *Learning to Walk in the Dark* (HarperOne, 2014).
Teilhard de Chardin, Pierre. *Christianity and Evolution* (Harcourt, 1974).
Tippett, Krista. *Speaking of Faith* (Penguin, 2008).
Weil, Simone. *First and Last Notebooks* (Wipf and Stock, 2013).
____. *Gravity and Grace* (Routledge, 2002).

———. *Simone Weil: Late Philosophical Writings* (Notre Dame, 2015).
———. *Waiting for God* (HarperPerennial, 1973).
Wiman, Christian. *My Bright Abyss* (FSG Adult, 2014).

www.ingramcontent.com/pod-product-compliance
Lightning Source LLC
Chambersburg PA
CBHW050550160426
43199CB00015B/2607